Simplified Entrepreneurship for Beginners

By:

Dr. John Michael Lao

Website: http://smartmoneypinoy.wixsite.com/main

Facebook: https://www.facebook.com/docmayhem/

For information about this book please contact 522-1144 look for Mrs. Joy

Or email drjmcl77@yahoo.com

Introduction

An entrepreneur is a person or group of people who engages in the creation and operation of a business or businesses. He undertakes the financial risks and responsibilities in search for solutions to problems which hopefully will result to a meaningful profit. Entrepreneurs are noble people for the impact they generate in society. They provide solutions for problems through skills, innovations and creative thinking. Imagine a life without a 24 hour sari-sari store / convenient store like (7-eleven or mini stop) which provides not only as a seller of goods and product but also provides other service like a prepaid phone loading station, cellphone charging station and as a Bayad Center where you can pay your house utility bills. These entrepreneurial innovations alleviates people of transportation cost to make payments for electricity or other utility bills convenient. They also helps you save precious time on long lines at payment centers.

A great entrepreneur once said that if you want to be a millionaire, you have to solve a million dollar problem. Philippines as a country is progressive but has a lot of industrial and technological flaws. These flaws can be turned into opportunities with the right entrepreneurial mindset. Another main feature of an entrepreneur is Job creation hence entrepreneurs are the life blood of society because without them there will not be any jobs and salaries to sustain members of the society.

If you look around your area you will notice that you are surrounded by different type of businesses. From the mall you go for shopping, the barbershop that cuts your hair, the electric company that provides your electricity, the TV station you watch at night and etc., they are all products of the entrepreneur's brilliant mind. These businesses are now providing jobs and salary for a lot of people. In fact most people with salaries are actually working for entrepreneurs.

Entrepreneurship is the process that the entrepreneur hurdlers to create a business enterprise. It involves activities like designing, launching and managing the business. Engaging in entrepreneurship involves facing multitude of risk. More than half of business fail or stagnate because of the inherent risk and problems in all type of business endeavor. That is why entrepreneurship is a hard task and a hard path to undergo. Many Great entrepreneurs will tell you the countless time they failed in business before they succeeded. It is imperative that you have to develop or acquire two of the greatest qualities of entrepreneurs, they are tenacity and adaptability. They are willing to challenge the odds of failure to reap the rewards. They are willing to disrupt the status quo to introduce a new innovation. They are willing to learn from their failures to improve and reinvent themselves for success.

In line with K to 12 Basic Education Program, this book was created for the benefit of Senior High school students and other business minded individuals who are interested in this field. This book will serve as an introduction to entrepreneurship as a viable career option. It will be more focus on the Small Business Operation (SBO) hence can be more relatable for high school student or budding entrepreneur. It is expressed in a simplified and comprehensible manner to be able to create and implement a proper business plan. This book will also introduce students to understand the different elements of business planning and business analysis. I hope by equipping beginners with knowledge, they can minimize risk and increase the like hood of business success. At the end, I hope that the student will have a self-evaluation or self-reflection if the life of an entrepreneur is the Path they are willing to undergo.

Table of Contents

BUSINESS PLANNING AND DEVELOPMENT PART

Chapter 1.

Planning a business

A business is an organization that involves supplying goods or service in exchange for monetary compensation. We as a society are surrounded and infused by business hence business is the life blood of our economy and a mechanism for money to flow between people.

An entrepreneur is a person or group of people who engages in the creation and operation of a business or businesses. In the creation of wealth the entrepreneur should be able to manage three main resources properly.

1. Natural resources – a good example of this is Land. If you have a land, you can get monetary compensation from it thru _RENT_.

2. Human resources – if you have manpower, you can get monetary compensation thru _LABOR._

3. Financial / Capital resources – if you have enough money, you can get monetary compensation thru _INTEREST._

If your goal is to be an entrepreneur, you have to consider the difference between an entrepreneur and an employee.

Difference between Employee and Entrepreneur

	Employee	Entrepreneur
income	Assured / limited	No assured / limitless
Working time	Usually 8 hours	Variable
investment	None	Highly invested
Financial risk	None	High financial risk
Work load	Stable	Variable (more workload particularly with start-up) Possibility of multi-tasking
Growth potential	Limited	Unlimited
motivation	Monetary stability (a few are passion driven)	Fueled primarily by passion and aspiration of

		unlimited financial possibilities
Personality	Usually Conformist	Innovators and independent
Retirement	60 above	None

Classification of small businesses

According to the Magna Carta for Micro, small and medium enterprises (R.A. No. 9501), their assets should belong to the following category.

Classification of MSME business based on assets

Business type	Lower limit	Upper limit
micro	Less than	3,000,000 Php
small	3,000,001 Php	15,000,000 Php
medium	15,000,001 Php	60,000,000 Php

Why are these information important to us? This Magna Carta for small enterprise or MSME are given important provisions the Government to support and to protect the development Micro Small and Medium enterprise. These support comes in skill development for labor, access for funding, government assistance, etc.

Barangay Micro-Business Enterprise Act 2002

- Micro-business enterprise may avail special incentives provided by the government thru R.A. 9178 or Barangay Micro-Business Enterprise act of 2002. The BMBE act of 2002 was signed by President Gloria Macapagal-Arroyo on November 13, 2002 to encourage the formation and growth of micro-businesses thru incentives and benefit.
- Incentives Include:
  - ➢ Tax exemption on income arising from the operation of the business enterprise
  - ➢ Exemption from the Minimum Wage Law
  - ➢ Priority to a special credit window setup specifically for the financing requirement of the BMBE

> ➤ Technology transfer, production training, management training, and marketing assistance for the BMBE beneficiaries.

- To register as a BMBE you should fall under the following criteria:
  > ➤ The business enterprise is engaged in production, processing, manufacturing of products, trading and services.
  > ➤ The business enterprise's total asset is 3,000,000.00Php or less including those arising from loans but excluding the land where the business and equipment used are located.
  > ➤ The business enterprise or service provider, in connection with his or her exercise of profession, is not a professional who is duly licensed by the government after having passed a government licensure examination (e.g. accountant, lawyer, doctor, etc.).

> The business enterprise is not a branch, subsidiary, division or office of a large scale enterprise or it is not a franchisee.

Go Negosyo Act 2014

The Act seeks to strengthen micro, small and medium enterprises (MSMEs) to create more job opportunities in the country. It was signed into law by the President Benigno S. Aquino III on 15 July 2014. The Department of Trade and Industry (DTI) issued Department Administrative Order (DAO) No. 14-5 Series of 2014: "Implementing Rules and Regulations for Republic Act No. 10644"

Types of small business based on activity:

1. Service – refers to the activity of providing service to customers for money. e.g. Barbershop, Car wash, Spa, etc

2. Manufacturing – refer to activity of creating a finish product from raw material. E.g. Cakes in bakery, electric power plant, Dried fruits manufacturer etc.

3. Wholesaling – refer to activity of buying a huge amount finished product for a discounted price and then selling them to retailers. E.g. Soft drinks wholesale storage facility.

4. Retailing – refers to the activity that sell product to end users. e.g. Sari-Sari store, appliance store, pharmacy, etc

5. **Mixed** – refers to a combination of 2 or more activities. E.g. cafe is a combination of manufacturing (they manufacture their own finish products like cooked pasta and brew coffee) and service (waiters or barista will serve them to clients)

Basic types of small business entity:

1. Sole propriety – is a business owned by one person. It has unlimited liability from its maker. Its governing agency is the Department of Trade and Industries.

2. Partnership – is a business owned by 2 or more persons. It has unlimited liability from its makers. Its governing agency is the Department of Trade and Industries.

3. Corporation – is a business owned by an artificial and individual entity created or incorporated by a group of people. Its entity has all the legal rights of a person that is separated from their makers. It has limited liability from its makers. Its governing agency is the Securities and Exchange Commission.

4. Cooperative - is similar to a corporation which is a business owned by an artificial and individual entity created by a group of 15 people with commonality. Its entity has all the legal rights of a person that is separated from their makers. It has limited liability from its makers. It also has tax privilege and government support as mandated by law with the purpose poverty alleviation. Its governing agency is the Cooperative Development Authority.

Chapter 2

Business Opportunities

Finding opportunity

Business opportunity are abundant in our everyday life. All you need is a critical mind, passion and gut feel for business. Upon the multiple of problems that surround our country, entrepreneurs discover business opportunities in solutions of innovation. A great entrepreneur once said if you want to be a millionaire, you must solve a million dollar problem.

Solutions of Innovations can come in many form:

1.	Invention of new product or service. E.g. the invention of Dengue vaccine to fight the pandemic occurrence of Dengue fever.

2.	Discovery of new and better processes. E.g. Bayad centers which are convenient and efficient solution for bill payment collections.

3. Substitution of cheaper alternative. E.g. generic medicine have the same effectivity as branded medicine but they are cheaper alternative.

4. Improvements of existing product. E.g. electric ovens with fermentation function, electric fan with mist function, or tooth picks with built-in dental flaws

5. New practical ways of using for existing technology. E.g used coffee grounds as organic plant fertilizer or used cooking oil for specialized electric generators.

A Sound Business Idea

A sound business idea is an economic opportunity which is within the reach of the entrepreneur and which will provide him with possible desirable returns. All entrepreneurs need a sound business idea to make a good business venture.

The process of creating a sound business idea and transforming it into a feasible business opportunity involves 4 stages:

1. **Decide on either establishing a start-up business or acquire an established business thru franchise.**

Difference between start-up business and franchise Business

	Start-up business	Franchise business
Control of the business	Full control	Some limitation
Payment of Royalties	None	yes
brand	You have establish your own brand	Established brand
Operational System support	You have to make your own system	Franchisor support
Cost to establish	Lower	Higher

Room for growth	Higher potential	limited
5 year success rate	43.8% (source:Sm allbiztrend. com)	95% (source: International franchisor Association)
Goals	Successful market entry	Successful market competition

2. How to make a List of Business idea

As in all type of business endeavor and research, everything starts with two methods:

a. Personal method.

This type of business idea is rooted from personal or vicarious experience. These type of method will generated business ideas based on your personal or your acquaintance's hobbies, skill, experience or work. E.g. a person who likes to cook or a person who had worked a long time in a professional kitchen might try to start his own restaurant.

Sample of personal method

Occupation / technical know-how	Personal motivation	Business Opportunity
Organic coffee Farmer	-Personal growth and financial stability	-Developing own organic coffee brand
Head Chef	-Culinary Creative freedom -full kitchen control	-establishing own restaurant

b. **Deliberate method.**

This type of business idea is rooted from a researched fundamental question like:

- ➤ What problems can I solve?
- ➤ How can I solve this problem?
- ➤ What does my target client need?

➢ What does my target client want?

➢ What can I offer my clients?

➢ How can I improve this product?

Sample of deliberate method

Researched Problem	Motivation	Business Opportunity
Electricity shortage in Barangay AB	- to improvement of the quality of life in Barangay AB	-Building an Electric cooperative in Barangay AB
Lacking of Quality and Clean drinking water in Barangay CD	-to improve the health of the citizens in Barangay CD	-establishing water purifying stations in Barangay CD

3. Screening of the Business Idea

Screening of business idea is a process choosing amongst your list of business ideas which can actually be feasible and profitable.

There a 4 major criteria for screening:

a. Marketable value.

You have to gather information and research on your idea to answer certain questions:

➢ Can you have sustainable and stable demand for you product?

➢ What is your product's competitive strength, weakness, opportunities and threats (SWOT analysis)?

Example of SWOT analysis

Strength	Weakness	Opportunity	threats
➢ Cost-effective Product.	➢ supply can't cope up with the demand	➢ increase the manpower to increase supply and sale	➢ Competitor's developing technology to improve efficiency
➢ good customer	➢ limited production		

relationship and support	and working capital	➢ technology training and support by government agency	➢ pending counter-productive government policies
➢ good and consistent quality control			

We can use information gathering techniques like literature review, interviews of potential clients, questionnaires, surveys and feedback forms.

b. Technical /operational viability.

The technical /operational aspect is one of the most important part of any business enterprise. It is responsible for the conversion of raw material or resource into finished product or service. In starting and operating a business, it is important that we should the technical skill-set to build and produce the product. If you don't have the technical knowledge, you either have to change your business idea to something you know or to get technical training from someone.

You should be able to answer certain questions like:

- ➢ Do you have the manpower to operate the business?
- ➢ Do you have the technical know-how regarding business operation and manufacturing?
- ➢ Do you have enough available raw material available?
- ➢ Do you have available machines for the conversion of raw material to finished product?
- ➢ Do you have enough electricity to power your machines?
- ➢ How can you transport the product to your customers?
- ➢ How can your customer buy your product?
- ➢ Are your products available on-line?

c. Capital build up.

A major aspect in starting a small business is building the source of funding for your business venture. You have to determine how much money you need to operate the business.

Your capital will be divided into 3 parts:

- ➤ *Pre-operative capital* – This capital includes cost that are related in the preparation for your business launch. It includes costs for feasibility study, market research, promotional cost and etc.

- ➤ *Production capital* – This capital includes costs for machine, computer, software, furniture, fixtures, structural modification of your facility and etc.

- ➤ *Working capital* – This capital includes cost for salary, account receivables, retainer fees, rentals, transportation, licenses and permit required, office supply, and etc.

You can start financing your business venture by the following:

- ➤ Personal savings
- ➤ Personal loan
- ➤ Angel investors
- ➤ Relatives and friends assistance
- ➤ Government assistance thru MSME loan program
- ➤ NGO assistance
- ➤ Bank loan for MSME

d. Profitability potential

Most entrepreneurial endeavor are profit driven. Without profit, business sustainability is impossible.

Profit is the monetary surplus after total cost are deducted from total revenue.

Profitability of a business can be established by 2 ways:

- ➤ ***Projected financial statements*** – are financial declaration that states thee prospective financial picture of the business. It includes projected balance sheet and income statement based on projected trends.

> ***Financial ratios*** – are financial tools used by businesses in determining the financial health of the company. With the financial ratio, we can get a picture of the financial strength and weakness of the company hence we are able to address the financial problems and provide alternative financial remedy.

4. **Final Selection / seizing the opportunity**

After careful consideration of the detailed process of turning a business idea to a feasible business opportunity. We must learn to choose the best business idea; it has to be the more profitable, less capital intensive, and more potentially sustainable for growth and development.

Sample Business proposal matrix

Business idea	Projected income	Less Capital Needed	Technical viability	Market value	total
Proposal A	4	2	4	3	13
Proposal B	4	5	4	4	17
Proposal C	3	3	2	5	13

(Assigned a value between 1 to 5; 1 being the lowest and 5 being the highest)

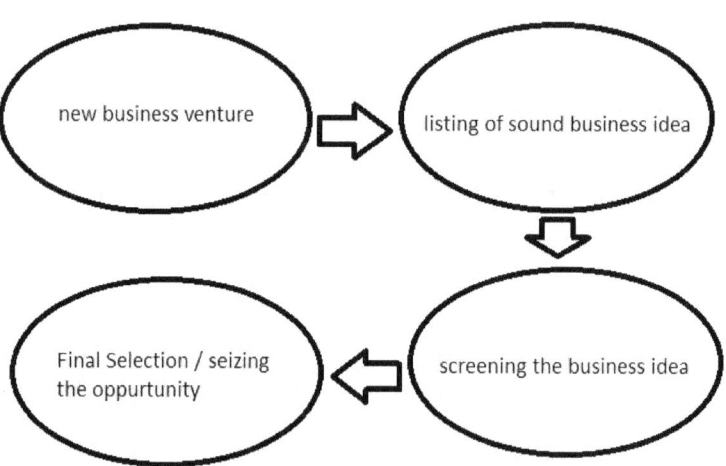

figure 2.1 Steps on Building a New Business venture from a sound business idea

Example of business ideas found in the DTI website:
http://www.dti.gov.ph/businesses/msmes/start-your-business#business-ideas

Example of SOAP Making Business

Herbal soap contains natural ingredients, juice or extract and vitamins from medicinal plants and fruits like papaya, lemon, and calamansi.

I. ESTIMATED INVESTMENT REQUIREMENTS

Tools/Equipment *

Materials	Cost
Glass or cup	P 295.90
Plastic pail (16 L capacity)	264.00
Cheese cloth or strainer	33.00
Wooden ladle or bamboo sticks	28.00
Knife	154.00
Chopping board	209.00
Plastic molders	963.00
Total	P 1,946.00

Materials/Ingredients *

Item	Qty	Cost
Caustic Soda (NaOH)	1 glass or 250 ml	P 12.10
Water	3 glasses	
Cooking oil	5 glasses	101.20
Juice or extract	½ glass	11.00
Total		P 124.30

*Based on 2012 market prices

II. PROCEDURES

1. Prepare the materials and the utensils needed.
2. Measure 1 glass of caustic soda and 3 glasses of water and pour into a plastic pail.
3. Mix well by stirring continuously using a wooden ladle or bamboo stick. Use only one direction when stirring.
4. Stir until the caustic soda is dissolved.
5. Pour 5 glasses cooking oil into the mixture.
6. Continue stirring until a consistency similar to a condensed milk is achieved then add ½ glass of juice or extract.
7. Pour the soap mixture into desired plastic molders.
8. Set aside and let it cool to harden.
9. After 4-5 hours, remove the soap from the molder.
10. Allow 30 days of ageing before packing.
10. Label the soaps.

Source: www.doh.gov.ph/pitahc/Herbal_Soap.html

Indications:
Kamias - fruit extract or juice (bleaching soap)
Calamansi - fruit extract or juice (bleaching soap)
Cucumber - fruit extract or juice (moisturizer)
Papaya - extract from fresh leaves (bleaching/ moisturizer)
Radish - extract from the stem (moisturizer)

III. ESTIMATED COSTING AND PRICING

Product Costing

Direct Cost

Particulars	Cost
Raw materials	P 124.30
Labor cost/5 times/formulation/day (P428/day min. wage)	85.20
Water and Electricity	50.00
Total Direct Cost	P 259.50

Indirect Cost

Particulars	Cost
Transportation Cost *	P 100.00
Total Indirect Cost	P 100.00

* May vary depending on distance between area of business operation and source of raw materials and/ or market area

Production Cost

Particulars	Cost
Total Direct Cost	P 259.50
Add: Indirect Cost	100.00
Estimated Production Cost	P 359.50

* Finished product will result in 15 bars of soap (130 grams/bar)

Product Pricing

Production cost per 130 grams soap	P 24.00
Add: 20% mark-up of the production cost	4.80
Estimated Selling Price/ 130 grams	P 28.80
Market Price per piece	P 30.00

* If price per 130 grams soap is lower compared with the existing market price, increase the mark-up to 30% or more. The higher the markup the higher the profit margin.

Chapter 3.

Market Study

Understand your market

Since you have learned how to come up with sound business idea, the next challenge is to understand your market and your competitors. You have define and isolate your target customers, identify your competitors and discover your competitive edge.

Market Research (target market, customers, market size)

Market research is the process of gathering, analyzing, and interpreting information about your prospective market and the product or service that you would like to offer. It includes Market Demographics, spending habits, location, and needs of the prospective market.

Accurate and comprehensive information is the key to a successful business enterprise because the knowledge of the market, competition, and the industry allows entrepreneurs to determine the feasibility of a business before committing a substantial amount of resources in a business idea.

With our market research, important information like Competitors, Market segmentation (identifying a segment of the market) and product differentiation (qualities of your product and service that are unique amongst your competitors) are possible.

Market research involves 2 types of informational data:

- Primary information

  If you gather information by yourself or hire someone to gather it for you. This includes observations research, and survey method (by interview, phone survey, email survey, and group survey).

- Secondary information

  If you use information that have been gather before by others. A good example of this using the data of the National Statistic Office, Local Government Unit, previous studies and etc.

✓ **Observational Method**

This type of correlational research in which a researcher observes a subject's ongoing behavior. It is particularly prevalent in social science and marketing studies. It is a social research technique that involves direct observation of phenomenon in a natural setting. The researcher or observer must be able to covertly hide himself so that the subject will not notice that he being observed.

➤ **Types of observational research:**

- **Covert observational research** - The researchers will not identify themselves; either they will mix themselves with the subject undetected, or they observe from a distance. The advantages of this approach are:

(1) Subject's cooperation is not a requirement

(2) The subjects' behavior will not be altered by the presence of the researcher.

- **Overt observational research** - The researchers purposely identify themselves to the subject and explain the purpose of their observations study. The problem with this approach is that the subject's behavior might be altered by the presence of the researcher. The advantage that the overt approach has over the covert approach is that there is no form of deception involved.

- **Researcher Participation** - The researcher participates in the study to get a finer appreciation of the phenomena and get a better perspective of the event.

Example on observational research

Situation 3.1

Product / service: Affordable and quality Eatery

Location: near barangay ABC surrounded by college A, B, and C

Target market: student and employee from College A, B, and C

Identifying the target: based on their school uniform

Observational Method: (record the following parameters)

1. Observe the students behavior during lunch time. Be gender specific

2. Where do they go to eat lunch? (Possible results: mixed group usually go to canteen 1, female customer usually go to canteen 2, male customer usually go to canteen3, college A student usually go to canteen 1, college B students usually go to canteen 3) These result will also help you identify your competitors.

3. What do they usually order? (to identify food preference of the different customers based on demographics)

4. How much do their meals cost? (to identify buying power of the different customers based on demographics)

5. Proximity of the other eatery from the school? (to assess the competition)

6. Observe other factors that attracts the customer to the other eatery? Are the personnel friendly and well groomed? How is the cleanliness of the place? Do they use coupon as incentives and rewards? What other promotional device do they use? (to assess competitor's edge)

✓ **Survey Method**

This method is the technique of gathering data and information by asking questions to your target market. A questionnaire is prepared. The respondents are asked questions on their demographic interest and opinion of proposed product and service. It can be done by face to face interview, telephone survey, and internet survey. The bigger the sample size means the better and more significant your result will be. You should collect you data and analyze data either by charts, tables and other statistical tool. With more computer software for making survey and data analysis easier, convenient and less tedious than before. Web applications like SurveyMonkey.com that can be linked to your social media platform and send to your targeted customers in an instant thru social media or emails.

❖ Advantages of Survey Method

- Surveys are effective to produce information on socio-economic characteristics, attitudes, opinions, and motives.

- They are effective in gathering information for planning product features, advertising media, sales promotion, channels of distribution and other marketing variables.

- Questioning is usually faster, and simpler to administer.

- It is easier to analyze, quote and interrelate the data obtained by survey method

❖ **Disadvantages of Survey Method**

- Some respondents have unwillingness to cooperate

- Inability of the respondents to provide information simply because of ignorance, technological log or socio-cultural log.

- Prone to human biases by the respondents.

Example on survey research

Situation 3.2

Product / service: Affordable and quality Eatery

Location: near barangay ABC surrounded by college A, B, and C

Target market: student and employee from College A, B, and C

Identifying the target: based on their school uniform

Survey Method: (ask the following question)

1. Demographic (record age, gender, school, year level, course/occupation, address, religion)
2. Where do you usually eat for lunch?
3. What is your usual order?
4. How much are you willing to spend for a meal?
5. What do would like to improve in your current restaurant?
6. What would you like to see in the menu?

✓ **Focus Group Discussion Method**

A focus group discussion is a gathering of selected people to participate in a planned discussion that is intended to elicit consumer perception about your prospected product or service in an environment that is non-threatening and receptive. The purpose for FGD is to collect information which will help in you tweak your product line and strategize marketing plan. The focus group method allows members of the group to interact and influence each other during the discussion and consideration of ideas and perspectives.

❖ What Contributes to Focus Group Success?

- **The quality of the focus group outcomes depends on the discussion**

  A good flow of discussion will lead to a good output for your focal group method.

  The focus group method is dependent on following factors to have a successful discussion:

  1. _Neutral and appropriate environment_ – the environment setting must be non-threatening for the participant.

  2. _Relatable product / service_ – your product should not be overwhelming for your participants. Don't choose men as participants in a Focus Group Discussion about menstrual pain medication.

3. _Participant selection_ – your objectives should be clear to be able to select proper participants. Participants are chosen based on their inclusion criteria as your target customer hence there are commonalities between them. If there is a mismatch between the participants, the discussion may be impeded. If you are start a Focus Group discussion about a new line of woman's executive and working outfit, you have to choose participant who are female, currently working in an office, more or less of similar income and educational attainment and etc.

4. _Select an effective facilitator_ – facilitator should create rapport with the participant to be able to facilitate a good and productive discussion. He should be kind, open, sensitive, receptive, flexible and objective-driven.

- **Participants must be guided properly towards the objective.** Facilitator should use interview guide or protocol that is predetermined and follows a logical sequence that is intended to mimic a natural exchange. Facilitators should avoid sudden changes of direction or topic, and they are careful to ensure that all participants in the focus group have equal input and contribution.

- **Focus group research findings are robust.** If the participants are genuinely engaged in the study and the moderator is sufficiently skillful, the outcomes are robust.

Chapter 4

Customer Profile

As entrepreneur, we can utilize our market research to create a database about our target customers to be used as a **guide for** determining what product and service is feasible to sell. These database are analyzed and correlated based on to their demographics, spending habits, life styles, motivations, preferences, and psychographics.

<u>Demographics profiles</u>

They are data on characteristic of selected population that are being used by a company for opinion or marketing research. Data includes age, gender, religion, income, occupation, educational attainment, residences and other demographic variables.

Example: If you are selling woman's clothes and accessories, you should try to research and determine the number of women, age distribution, and average earnings of your target market area.

<u>Marketing research use demographic to achieve certain objectives</u>:

- To determine what segment or subgroups exist in the overall population.

- To create a clear picture of the characteristics of the members of each subgroup.

- To be able to benefit from demographic data for the increase of product identification and product sale.

<u>Psychographic segmentation</u>

They are information that defines your buyer's habits, motivations, spending habits, lifestyle, personal traits, degree of loyalty, and occasions. This a powerful tool to market a product to the different segments of the population. A good psychographic data of your buyer can lead you to better understanding of your client. It will affect marketing approach, product development and opportunity seeking strategies thru the other segment of the population.

Example: a good strategy commonly implemented by various shopping malls is the "PAY-DAY weekend sale". This strategy capitalizes on the customer's spending habit during payday.

Technographic segmentation.

With the advent of **personal computer, tablets, smart devices, robotics** and other technological advancement, the population was classified based on the level of expertise in the use of technology. Since the boom of the internet era, internet marketing became more global and efficient that internet advertising can provide their own analytics. Market researchers realized the need for a segmentation scheme based on the role that technology plays in consumers' lives.

Example: Recent retailers have been using on-line platform to sell their product because it increases their market coverage and market segment.

Market Mapping

A study of the various market conditions that is plotted on a map to identify different market trends and variables between consumers and products. Data on demographic segmentation, psychographic segmentation, and technographic segmentation can be utilized for this purpose. It will give us a better visual illustration of the current market and it will give us cues on possible "Gap in the current MARKET".

The "***Gap in the current Market***" is a gap between the <u>needs and want of customers</u> as well as the <u>product present in the current market</u>.

The market map illustrates the range of "positions" that a product /service can take in a market based on two dimensions that are important to customers.

Examples of those dimensions might be:

- High price vs low price

- Basic quality vs High quality

- Low volume vs high volume

- Necessity vs luxury

- Light vs heavy

- Simple vs complex

- Lo-tech vs high-tech

- Young vs Old

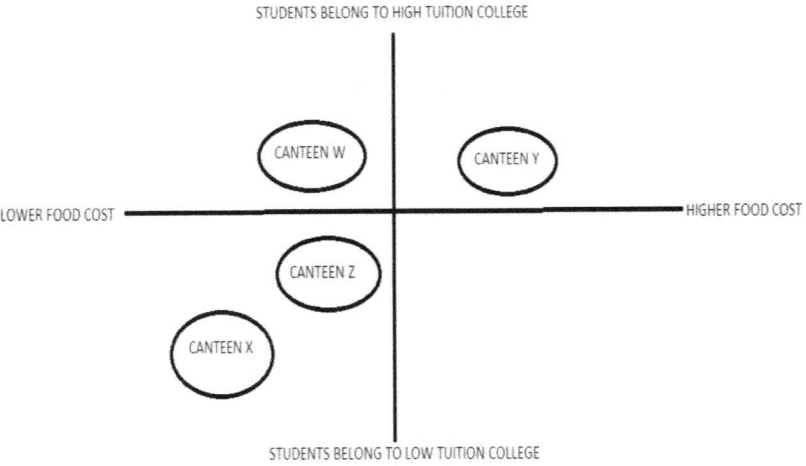

FIGURE 3.1 MARKET MAPPING ON CANTEENS BASED ON FOOD COST VS STUDENTS TUITION FEE

Chapter 5

PRODUCT DEVELOPMENT

For entrepreneurs, business products are any goods, services, or idea that can be offered to target customers that satisfy their needs and want in exchange for money or some unit of value.

Product development refers to systematic process of all aspects of development and management of a product. Product are always developed because there are "Gaps in the current market". This gaps need to be filled. This "Gap in the current market" is an Entrepreneurial opportunity for us to capitalize and make some money along the way.

For a Product to be successful it must have the following:

- It must be desirable to the target market
- It must answer a "GAP in the current Market"
- It must have a competitive edge against other product
- It must be unique

What are the 8 stages of product development?

1. **Idea generation** – an invention or innovation that results from trying to bridge the gap between the needs and want of a customer against a solution or product to fill that void. The act of conceptualizing a product that is not currently available in your target market is biggest challenge.

    Example: Fast Food was developed to answer a GAP between people's immediate hunger and the lack of time or skill of people in preparing a meal.

2. **Idea screening** – there is a great need to screen your ideas because it is a known fact that not all ideas are feasible and good ones. We should try to introduce the idea to target customers and assess if they are going to be receptive in using the conceptualized product.

Example: coke introduce cherry coke in the Philippines but unfortunately Filipinos were not receptive to the idea unlike westerners.

3. **Concept development and testing** – once you receive a good feedback, now is the time for you to develop a "prototype".

A prototype a sample or model of your product built to test a concept or process or to act as a thing to be replicated or learned from.

This prototype is then used or sampled by your target market so you can assess if the product is working and so you can get feedback on how to improve it.

Example: if you are planning to open a cupcake shop, you should start prototyping different flavor and design of cupcake for field testing or taste testing, then get the feedback from your customers on how to improve your cupcake and what flavor is most delicious and visual pleasing for them.

4. **Market strategy** – this stage is about developing your marketing strategies. You have to address the marketing mix.

The marketing mix strategy was devised by E. Jerome McCarthy and published it in his book called Basic Marketing. It is a tool used by Entrepreneurs in assessing and defining key issues regarding the product or brand offering.

It is composed of the 7 P's:

*   **Product** – this is the product that you have designed. Is your product a working product? Is it at par with the client's expectation? Is it a product that the customer will want? Are these the right products and services for our customers today? What is the difference between your products from the other competitors?

- **Place** – this will reflect the accessibility of your product by your target market and customers. Availability of your product will depend on the following:

✓ Wholesaler

✓ Retailers

✓ Own store

✓ Direct sales

✓ Online market

✓ Mail order

Is the product accessible for your client? Do you have proper delivery system and logistics? Can you order thru e-commerce or internet purchasing? Where else can you offer your product?

- **Price** – this is about putting the right price for your product.

There are different ways to come up with the right price. They are:

- ✓ Cost plus – total cost of the product plus % mark up
- ✓ Consumer led – researching your customers buying power and producing a product that they would consider a fair price.
- ✓ Competitive – pricing your product based on the existing competition
- ✓ Penetration – entering the market with low price, then once you get market acceptance you can raise your product's price gradually.
- ✓ Skimming – initially high price upon entering the market but gradually decreasing the price over time secondary to lowering of production cost overtime.
- ✓ Premium – high pricing that reflects a luxury brand
- ✓ Economy – lower pricing to target increase sales volume

How much are the target client willing to pay for your product? Is your price competitive? Is your price good value for money?

- **Promotion** – This is how the customer finds out about your product. It's about the following:

✓ Advertising

✓ Public relations

✓ Sponsorship

✓ Sales promotion

✓ Social media promotions

How are going to promote it? Are you going to use social media? Is your promotion directed to your target clients? Are you prepared to modify your marketing and promotional strategy based on the current trends?

- **People** – this are people involve in selling your product and supporting your company. Do you have right people to run your business?

- **Packaging**- this how your client will see your product. Is your product or service packaged in an aesthetically appealing manner? Will your client enjoy the experience of using your product?

- **Positioning** – how does your product position itself in the market field. How do your client feel, think and talk about your product? Is the product your offering to your clients a good deal? Does your product leave a good impression on your clients?

5. **Feasibility analysis** – this stage often overlap with other stages. This is an analysis and evaluation of a proposed project to determine the following:
   - ✓ If the project is technically feasible. Do you have the technical capacity to produce the product
   - ✓ If we can have the raw material to produce the product
   - ✓ If we have the manpower to run the company
   - ✓ If we can keep the project within a reasonable cost

✓ If we have distribution channel to make the product available to the consumer

✓ If we can promote the product at a reasonable cost

✓ If the project can give us a reasonable profit

6. **Product technical design** – this stage is a collaboration between the feasibility analysis and the customer's feedback. We don't only aim for a functional product, we have to also design the product that might be aesthetically pleasing or ergonomic for our consumer.

The design will depend on 2 major things:

- Its functionality
- It should be at par with customer's expectation

Example: a customer will not only buy your cupcake because it's delicious, they will also buy it because it is visually appetizing and beautiful.

7. **Test marketing** – at this stage, we test the acceptance of the product. This occurs when try to sell the product to random people of your target market, then we ask them for their feedback and comment. The consumer feedback will be used to improve your product and it will determine if you are going to continue to the next stage.

Example: Before you start selling your cupcake, try a food tasting event and assess if the market will accept your cupcake.

8. **Market entry** – this is the stage when our product officially enters the market. We will try sell it to everyone that belongs to our target market. This the time when the product's life cycle begins. The product's life cycle will be determined by your consumers, competition, and product advancement. Without these 3 elements (<u>consumer patronage, competitive edge and product advancement)</u> our product's life cycle will end.

Chapter 6

Funding Your Business

One of the most important question in starting a business enterprise is the financial funding of a business venture. With this dilemma, most budding or beginning entrepreneurs begin to get discouraged and frustrated. As an entrepreneur, you have to hurdle this stage to get to the next level. Remember that every entrepreneurial endeavor can either succeed or worst fail hence we always prepare and plan for a business enterprise to decrease the chance of failure and increase the like-hood of success. In the advent of internet, more information and technological breakthroughs has appeared particularly for funding a MSME or small businesses.

The fundamental question is "HOW DO WE FUND OUR BUSINESS?". Fortunately there are a lot of ways to fund a business venture. Our government has made efforts making Philippines a business friendly country for a reason.

The government wants an increase of business creation in our country therefore increasing employment for Filipinos.

These are the ways to fund a business venture:

➤ **FUND IT YOUR SELF**.

1. If you have enough savings and cash at hand, you can fund the project yourself.

2. Try to looking around and assess what you own that has monetary value. You might have old clothes, computer, and smart phone or tablet that you have not been using for a few years and sell it to fund your business venture.

3. You might try to get a job to gain some starting capital. Just remember to make sure you have enough before you start a business because it is difficult to get additional funds in the middle of business creation stage.

➤ **LOANS AND MICRO-FINANCE**

You can start barrowing money thru institutional Loan providers. There are a lot of financial institution that lend money to small business particularly MSME businesses. They may come in attractive interest rates or special rate for MSME as micro-financial loans. Here are some of the example:

- ✓ The Fico Bank offers the Kabayan microloan for entrepreneurs.

- ✓ The Bangko Kabayan Inc. offers both microfinance loans and an SME loan.

- ✓ The Cantilan Bank Inc. offers microfinance loans a business finance loan.

- ✓ Fairbank offers microfinance loans and SME loans.

➢ **CROWDFUNDING** – it is the practice of funding a project or a venture by collecting small amounts of money from a lot of people, usually through the Internet. There are crowd funding site for the Philippines.

✓ <u>Fundko.com</u> is a crowd funding site that support Filipinos who need money for a particular project.

✓ <u>Homegrown.ph</u> is a Filipino crowd funding community.

✓ <u>Start Some Good</u> is an Australia based global crowdfunding platform for social impact projects.

➤ **ANGEL INVESTMENT**

There are a lot of people in the metropolitan area with enough money to invest in a good business idea. Usually they come together in a group called Angel Network. You can have access to them thru the following ways:

1. You can group together and present your business plan to your family and relatives.

2. You can access angel investors thru online platforms like:

   ✓ Idea Space Foundation' program is intended to provide startups the support needed at critical phases when ideas are being turned into actual commercial products

   ✓ 500.co is a Seed funding body that funds companies all around the world, including the Philippines.

   ✓ Philippines Angel Investors is a list of private angel investors active in the Philippines.

   ✓ Manila Angels is a Manila (Philippines) based private network of Angel investors.

➢ **GRANTS**

You can also apply for business grants from different company more particularly if your business contains components of social impact. Here are some examples:

1. <u>Manila-based Asian Development Bank (ADB)</u> is offering an initial $3.6-million grant for the development of inclusive business in the Philippines and the rest of Asia.

2. <u>The Asian Information Society Innovations</u> Fund offers grants in Internet Based Solution related innovations.

3. <u>QBO</u> the Philippines first innovation Hub that provides free platform and facility for start-up business and technopreneurs. It provides programs, lectures and free consultations to accelerate the incubation of a business. This program was established in partnership of DOST, J.P. Morgan and Idea Space foundation. It also provide an access for start-up businesses to various investors interested in funding and supporting a financially feasible business opportunity. It is the Silicon Valley of the Philippines.

Recent interest by our legislators on promoting MSME hence pushing laws providing tax incentives and tax holidays for budding start-up businesses. These government endeavors increases the chances for a start-up's success.

Chapter 7

Financial Data

This area of business is essential and important for us to understand. We need to visualize and predict the financial wellbeing of a business. Doctors will check vital signs to assess patient's health status while entrepreneurs and financial expert will definitely check the financial data of a business to assess its financial situation. I know that some students might try to skip this chapter because of the Math involved and it might be their waterloo but Financial Data are functional math. It will make the difference between profit and loss. You will need some time to understand it but I will try to make it as simple as possible.

Figure 7.1 Entrepreneur using Financial Data

Remember that our objective is not to try to make you an expert accountant rather just make you aware and understand enough financial information for you to roughly assess the financial risk involved in engaging or investing in an entrepreneurial venture.

➢ **INCOME STATEMENT**

It is a financial statement that presents a company's financial performance over a specific accounting period of time. It will show the company's revenue and cost which vital for us to access the financial strength of the company. It is also called *Profit and Loss statement* or *revenue and expense statements.*

Some of the items included in the income statement are the following:

1. ***Gross Annual Sales***. It is the total revenue or sale that your company have accumulated in a year

2. ***Cost of Goods sale***. These are direct cost that are attributed to the production of your product and service. (Raw materials, Direct Labor cost, and etc.)

3. ***Gross Profit***. the difference between Gross Annual Sales and Cost of Goods sales

4. ***Selling, General and Administrative Cost***. These are cost that incur which are not directly attributed to the manufacturing of product and service. (selling expense, promoting expense, distribution cost, rent, utilities, mortgage, wages, administrative expense, warranties, insurances, and etc)

5. **Operating Income**. The difference between Gross Profit and Selling, General and Administrative Cost. This an income incur from the operation of the company.

6. **Net income**. The difference between the Operation income and Taxes.

Example# 7.1

Marie's Flower Shop

Income statement

For the Year ending Dec. 31, 2016

Gross Annual Sales	800,000	
Less:		
Cost of Goods Sold		
Seeds	50,000	
Fertilizer	20,000	
Labor	200,000	
Mineralized	10,000	
Water		520,000
Gross Profit		
Less:		

SGA	60,000	
Rent	100,000	
Salary	50,000	
Insurance	30,000	
Utilities	20,000	
promotional		260,000
Operating income		
Less:	30,000	
Taxes		230,000
Net Profit:		

> **BALANCE SHEET**

It is an accounting tool that serve as a financial statement of assets (what we own), liabilities (what we owe) and equities (Net assets/net worth) at a particular period of time. It is also called a "snap shot" of a company's financial condition.

It is broken up into 3 sections

ASSETS	LIABILITIES	EQUITIES

The formula ASSETS – LIABILITIES = EQUITIES

The Assets (what we own)

The assets are valuable things that a company owns. It has been divided into 2:

a. <u>Current assets</u> are cash or any valuable properties that can reasonably converted to cash within a year.

Includes:

➢ Cash

➢ account receivables (money to be received from customers)

➢ inventory (list of goods to be sold)

➢ prepaid expenses (future expenses that have paid in advance)

b. <u>Non-current assets / Long term assets</u> are assets that in not likely to be turned into cash within a year.

Includes: Factory, Equipment, building, and etc.

The Liabilities (what we owe)

The Liabilities are company's financial debt or obligations that arises during the course of business operation. It has been divided into 2:

a. Current liabilities are amount due to paid to creditors with the year

   Includes:

   ➤ Accounts payable (sum to paid to supplier)

   ➤ Accrued expenses (refers to operational expenses like payroll, overhead expense)

   ➤ taxes

b. Non-current liabilities / Long term liabilities are long term financial obligation that are not due to paid to creditors with the year.

   Includes:

   ➤ Bonds payable (forms of long term debt and bonds are usually issued by a company to barrow money from investors to be paid with interest)

➢ Mortgage payable (refers to loans for buying real estate)

The Owners Equity (Net assets/net worth)

The Equity refers to the amount of funds contributed by the _shareholder / owners_ plus _Retained income_ (net earnings not paid out as dividend, but are retained by the company to be reinvested to the core business or to pay debt).

Example # 7.2   BALANCE SHEET ILLUSTRATION

ED's delivery service

If you are starting a delivery services and you barrowed an amount of 500,000 from bank.

ASSETS	LIABILITIES	EQUITIES
Cash (500,000)	Loan (500,000)	

Then you decide to buy a motorcycle as a delivery vehicle worth 300,000.

ASSETS	LIABILITIES	EQUITIES

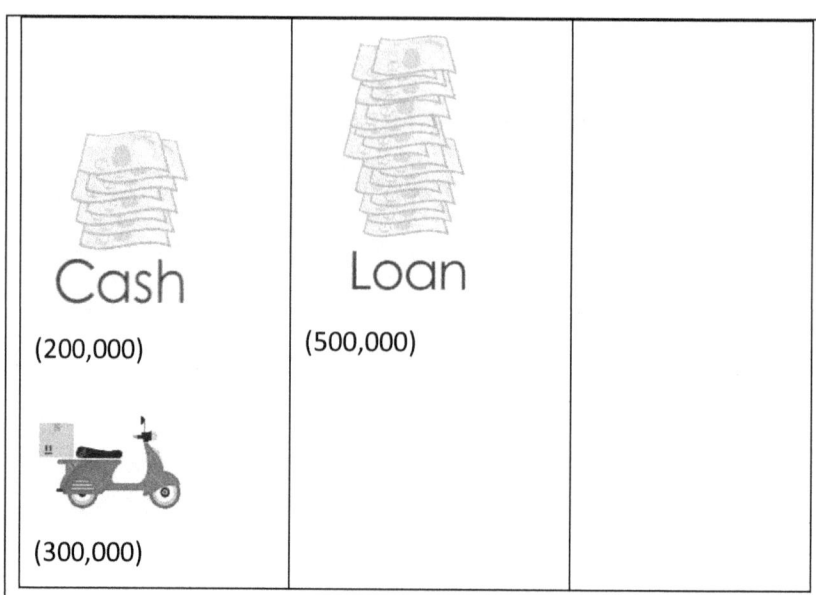

Cash	Loan	
(200,000)	(500,000)	
(300,000)		

Then you start your business delivering product for people and made a profit of 300,000. This will be recorded a retained earnings

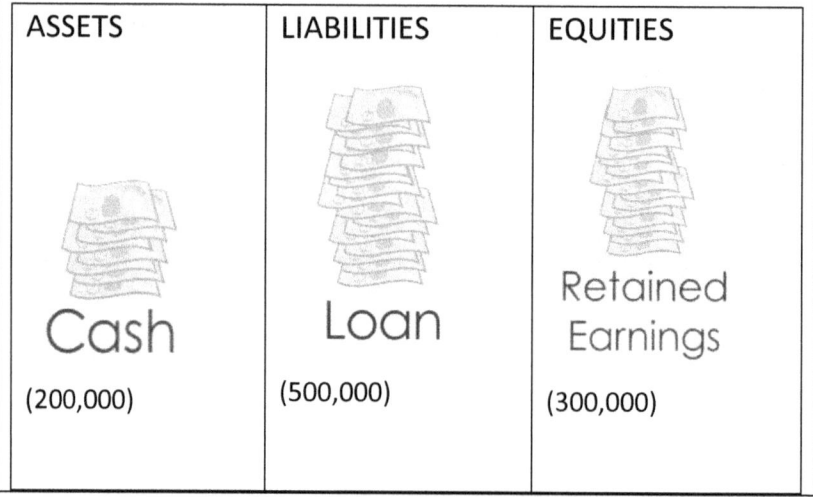

ASSETS	LIABILITIES	EQUITIES
Cash	Loan	Retained Earnings
(200,000)	(500,000)	(300,000)

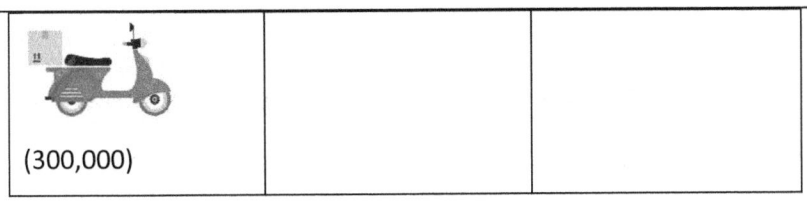(300,000)		

Then cash profit will be added to you to Cash section under ASSETS

ASSETS	LIABILITIES	EQUITIES
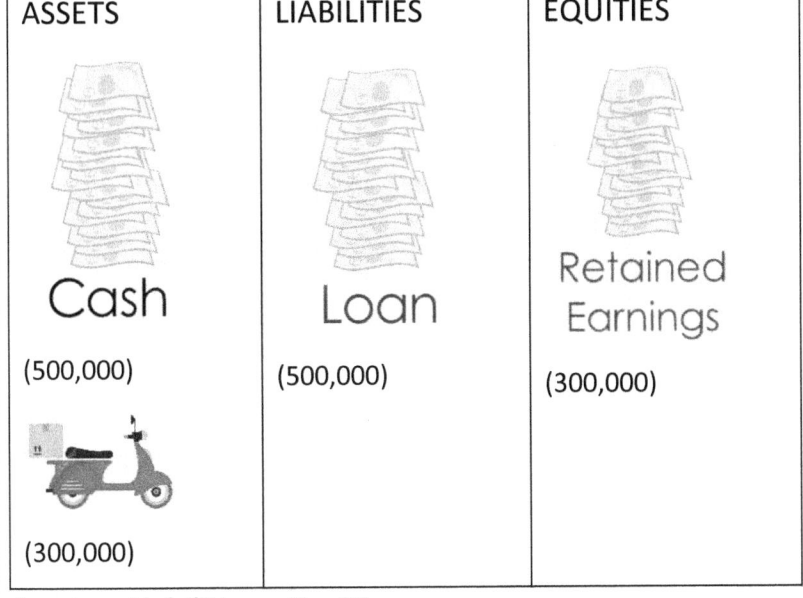Cash (500,000) (300,000)	Loan (500,000)	Retained Earnings (300,000)

Assets – Liabilities = Equities

800,000 – 500,000 = 300,000 (everything is balanced in the balance sheet)

Then after 1 month you have to pay your monthly bank loan 200,000 hence your cash will decrease as well as your liabilities

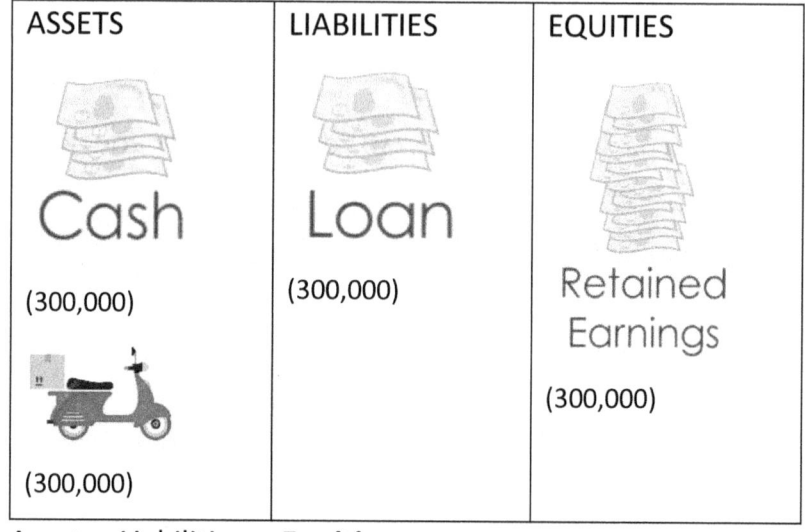

ASSETS	LIABILITIES	EQUITIES
Cash (300,000)	Loan (300,000)	Retained Earnings (300,000)
(300,000)		

Assets –Liabilities = *Equities*

600,000 – 300,000 = ***300,000***

Example #7.3

Ed's delivery service balance sheet
December 31, 2016

Assets	
Cash	150,000
Account receivables	25,000
Inventories	75,000
Prepaid Expense	50,000
Net Fixed Assets	300,000
Total ASSETS	600,000
Liabilities and Owners equity	
Notes Payable	50,000
Accounts Payable	50,000
Accrued Liabilities	50,000
Long term debt	150,000
Total Liabilities	300,000
Owner's Equity	300,000
Total Liabilities and Owner's Equity	600,000

Cash Flow Statement

It is a statement that reports the cash generated and utilized during a specific period in time. It is used to capture both operating results and the accompanying changes in a balance sheet. It can also be used to determine short term viability of a company, particularly in paying its bills.

Cash flow reports the inflow and outflow of cash thru the following categories:

- Operating Activities. These constitute revenue generating activities of the business. (e.g. product sale, royalties, commissions, suppliers and lenders invoices and payroll)
- Investing Activities. These contains payment made to acquire long term assets. (e.g. purchasing of fixed assets, and purchasing or selling of securities issued by other companies)
- Financing Activities. These are activities that will alter the equity and borrowing of a company. (e.g. sales of company shares, repurchase of company shares, and dividend payments)

The following items are included in the cash flow statements

1. Cash (cash on hand)
2. Cash sales (cash from sales)
3. Receivables (income from credit sales)
4. Other income (income from other investments or securities, loan interest,)
5. Total income (sum of income)
6. Materials and merchandise (raw material, supplies used for company's operation)
7. Direct labor (Labor for manufacturing and service)
8. Overhead (all fixed and variable expenses for the day to day operation of the business)
9. Marketing expenses (expenses that involves marketing your product)
10. Research and development (expenses that support the R and D to improve your product or service hence necessary for product advancement)
11. General and Administrative expenses (expenses that support the general and administrative function of

the company. These expense are not really directly tied to the manufacturing, production and sales. E.g. accounting staff salary, building rent, depreciation of fixtures and equipment, wages of executives, insurances, legal counsel, office supplies, and etc.)

12. Taxes (refers to all types of taxes except for payrolls withholding tax)

13. Capital (fund needed to purchase equipment needed to generate income)

14. Loan payments (include payment for loan)

15. Total expenses

16. Cash flow (the difference between income and expenses)

17. Cumulative cash flow (the difference between cash flow from the current year to the previous year)

Example #7.4		
Sample of Cash Flow Statement		
Ed's Delivery service		
Projected cash flow		
2016-2017		
	2016	2017
Cash sales	250,000	300,000
Receivables	80,000	150,000

Other income	10,000	5,000
Total income	340,000	455,000
Materials	50,000	70,000
Direct labor	50,000	60,000
overhead	10,000	50,000
Marketing and sales	10,000	8,000
Research and	10,000	20,000
development	50,000	55,000
General and	2,000	3,000
administrative	20,000	20,000
Taxes	8,000	8,000
Capital	210,000	294,000
Loan	130,000	161,000
Total Expenses	0	291,000
Cash Flow		
Cumulative Cash flow		

The cash flow is a simple tool that must be carefully examined and presented in all business plan. It will show if there is a positive or negative prospect to gain profit and sustainability of a project. If the results turns out negative therefore it is not a feasible investment.

Chapter 8

Business Plan

What is a business plan?

A business plan is a formal document that states a business goals, business viability, and business strategy to attain them. It is the ultimate blueprint of a business. It will ultimately show you the goals, the business direction, and financial forecast of a potential business venture. In this Chapter of the book, we will try to simplify and collaborate the knowledge from the other chapters. This chapter will provide you with basic skill set to able to write a simple business plan.

figure 8.1 Business Plan

According to a research made by Palo Alto Software, Entrepreneurs who finished their business plan were about twice as likely to grow their business, get investment or land an investment deal. (http://timberry.bplans.com/real-data-on-the-success-of-business-planning.html)

The purpose of writing a business plan if as follows:

1. **To secure funding for a business**

   This is a formal document required by lending institution for an entrepreneur who is asking them for a business loan. This is also requirement by investors to assess if they want to invest in your business because it will give them a mental and financial picture of the business.

2. **To guide business managers on the direction of the business**

   It will help managers and supervisors to understand the goals, vision, and direction of the business. It will also highlight the operational part of the business. It can be referred as an instructional manual or a bible of your business. Some company even ask their employee to memorize the company's mission and vision because it will help employee realize the objective of the company.

3. **To be utilized as a reference guide if the business needs recalibration**

Business plan are used by entrepreneurs in recalibration and assessing the direction of a business. It keeps your business in the right track. We can use it to assess the reasons why company goals are not achieved hence implementation of revisions and alterations in the business plan are needed.

From time to time the business plan of a particular business changes based on the objective of the present business condition. For example: the business plan that you used when you started the business might not be applicable if you are going to diversify and grow your business.

PARTS OF A BUSINESS PLAN:
✓ Title page and content

This should include business name, people that contributed, date, and the address, contact information (telephone number, fax number, email, and website) and the writer of the business plan

✓ Executive summary

The executive summary is the summary of the whole business plan. It is analogous to the abstract in a research study. This part should be concise to attract the attention of the reader. Usually it is better to complete the other parts of the business plan first while leaving the executive summary last. It should include a brief nature of the business, capitalization, profit generation, and sustainability.

✓ Business description

In this part, you are given a chance describe your business. What is your mission and vision? What does your business do? Business ownership or the kind of business entity planned? Target Customers? Distribution strategy? These questions will allow you to tell the story behind the business.

✓ Product or service Description

This is the part of the business plan that we have to describe the product or service that we are selling. How do you manufacture your product? How do we use the product? What problems does it solve? What gives our product the competitive edge? What are the result of your SWOT analysis?

✓ Market Strategies

This part of the business plan is a discussion on your market strategy based the fundamental of market research. How can you benefit from of the existing market? How will you enter the market? How do you position yourself in the market? How is your price and pricing strategy? How will you promote your product? How will you distribute your products?

✓ Analysis of the competition

To be able to assess if the market will buy your product, you should be able to study your competition. By identifying and understanding your competitor's product and processes, you will be able to develop a better product. You can showcase your competitive advantage in this segment. Who are your competitors? What makes your product better than others? What can convince your target customers to shift and your product? What are your competitor's strengths and weaknesses? What are your competitor's market strategies?

You be able to use comparative tables like table 8.1.

Table 8.1 An Comparative table between Marvin's Café and competition's product

	Marvin's café	Company A	Company B	Company C
Coffee Beans used	Local bean + Ethiopian blends	Brazil's beans	Ethiopian beans	Columbian beans
Flavor	Bold and sweet	Bold and sweet	Sweet	robust
Coffee of choice based on Blind taste challenge of 500 participants	104 (20.8%)	127 (25.4 %)	140 (28%)	129 (25%)
Cost	1 pesos per gram	5 pesos per gram	10 pesos per gram	5 pesos per gram

Marketing Strategy	Prospective Agreements with Airports and Call centers café	Tie up with mid-range malls	Tie up with high end malls	Tie up standalone café
Sales team	3 years of experience	7 years of experience	>10 years of experience	10 years of experience
Ages of primary target clients	35 ± 7 years old	40 ± 7 years old	50 ± 5 years old	43 ± 5 years old

✓ Operation and management

The operations and management plan will describe how your business functions on a day to day basis. This section will highlight the organization chart or structure that will describe how each and every member of the company will function as to their duties and obligation to the company. It will also highlight the capital (pre-operative capital, production capital and working capital) and expense requirements (operating expenses and cost of goods sold) related to the operations of the business.

This segment is also important to show the expertise and qualifications of each member of the team in your organizational chart. In a basketball team, you should know every one of your players. Investors usually look at the key players of a business and use that to assess either to invest or not to invest in your company.

✓ Financial data

This segment of the business plan highlights the financial aspect of the company. Since financial managers of investment companies are more interested on the numbers of the company hence we have to illustrate the story of our company thru numbers. Financial data section should display profit generation, financial sustainability, and potential financial growth. These business characteristics can be demonstrated properly by presenting your Balance sheet, financial income statement, and cash flow projection.

✓ Supporting Document

Finally, you should be able to provide supporting documents towards your claim. This segments contain the owner's resume, references from supplier and retailers, client list, lease or rental agreement, tax returns, previous income statements, patents and copyright and etc.

Chapter 9.

Business Implementation

Business implementation is the process of carrying out a business plan so that business concept becomes a business reality. The Burden of business implementation rest on the shoulder of all the employees. To implement the business plan correctly, supervisors and managers should communicate the company's goals, mission, vision and expectations to their employees. These will give an internal compass of what the company is aiming for. The company should also provide their employees with the resources needed to help the company achieve its goals. This is applicable to a new business or to an existing business

Business implementation brings about 3 major event.

a. **Change**

Business implementation of a plan brings about change for the development or improvement of a company and its function. We also need change to solve a business problem. The change may occur at any part of the business process. They may include changes in the company policies, company budgets, management and organizational structure, and manufacturing process of products or services. A business should constantly change and develop to improve their product and service for a total customer satisfaction

b. Company development

If a business shares its goals, mission and vision to its employees, the employees will feel a certain bond, sense of loyalty and a sense of purpose coherent with the company. We have to utilize these internal motivations for the improvement of the organization.

c. Clarifies company priorities

When the company communicates the goal and objective to employees, the priorities of the companies are clarified. The company express their realistic expectations towards deadlines, client's needs, employee's needs, financial targets and company's growth prospects. To be able to achieve all these expectation, we need the participation of all the employee in business implementation.

Mission and Vision

➢ Mission statement.

A Mission statement focuses on the present and near future. It explain the product or service offered, the target customers, and company's expectation on its service. It outline the shared purpose of all the stakeholders. It answers questions like: Where we are now? Why we do what we do? Who benefits from what we do? What makes us different from others?

➢ Vision statement.

A vision statement focuses on the future. It is a source of motivation and inspiration. It will describe the future prospect of the company 10-15 years from now. It is reflective of the internal purpose and the values of the business.

Table 9.1 Mission and vision of **Bureau of Immigration Philippines**

OUR VISION
We are committed to provide the most efficient, innovative and effective immigration service.
OUR MISSION
To control and regulate the movement of persons to, from and within our country in contributing to national development.

Source: http://www.immigration.gov.ph/the-bureau/vision-and-mandate

Business Aims and Objective

Business aims are the long term goals that assist us in the formulation of our business objectives. This can usually be found in the Mission statement. It answers the question: what is the company aiming for? To be able to achieve our business aims, we have to set up our objectives.

Business objectives are long term to medium term goals of a company. It has to be attainable and realistic for all the employees working to achieve them. If the business objective is unrealistic, it will give more pressure to the employee causing intense workforce frustration. A good solution to this problem is ask a consultation and compromised agreement with the employees on what a realistic objective entails. It will also promote a sense of responsibility and bond between the company and employee hence motivating employees toward a higher level of productivity.

Example of business of objective are to increase profit, production, or improvement in the service of the company toward a long term company growth.

To summarize <u>Aims</u> are long term ambitions of the company while <u>objectives</u> are realistic company steps to achieve those ambitions.

Business Strategy

Business Strategies are courses of action that will serve as a guide for a company toward achieving its business objective. It will direct the company's effort and energy on the details of what the company need, what the company should do to address those needs, who are involved in the solution and when do we execute the contemplated solution.

Table 9.2

AIMS, OBJECTIVE, and STRATEGIES

of MARVIN's café

Aims	Objectives	Business strategies
To be the # 1 supplier quality Blended coffee beans in NCR.	1.To increase production coffee beans by 50% in 2017	1.Increase partnership program with local farms all around Philippines particularly in the Malaybaylay and Bukidnon coffee farms. 2.Increase 3 more coffee roasting facilities

		3.Increase importation of Ethiopian Beans by 50% within the year
	2.To increase market presence in NCR	1.Increase 10 more representative office around NCR 2.increase existing clients and prospective client meeting by 20% per month.
	3.To increase sales by 20% in 2017	1.Increase sales manpower by 10%. 2.Allocate experienced and reputable sales people from the main office to supervise and train new representative office around NCR. 3.create new promotional sales and

		terms of payment for customers. 4.re-evaluate the logistic and the sale route of each sales representative to achieve efficiency.

What is the importance of a Business Name?

A business name is a big endeavor in starting a business. A bad name can mean disaster for a business. If you apply behavioral psychology in marketing, your customer should associate your business name with a good product and a good customer experience.

Here are a few tips in coming up with a name:

1. Good recall.

   Make sure your name can be easily recalled by people. People should remember your business name so it can easily be associated with the type of service and product you are marketing.

2. Make it Simple

   You don't need to make your name complicated with abbreviations, unusual spellings or characters, and excessively long name.

3. Covey your service.

   You should choose a name that will give your target customers a glimpse of what your business is offerings.

4. Captured market.

   You should not give a name that limits your target market hence limiting your sales and growth potential.

5. Business name availability

   You have to make sure the name you want is available. You can check the name availability thru the DTI or SEC.

6. Survey your name

   You can make a survey asking your target market to rank between the 5-10 names that you came up with. The survey should result to a business name that is most appealing and most reflective to the type of business you have.

Chapter 10

Human Resources Management

Human resources department is a section of your company that deals with finding, screening, hiring, training, compensation evaluation and terminating employees.

It is essential for a company to have a Human Resources Department because they are responsible for hiring the right people for the right job. Having the right people in place, the productivity and the efficiency of a company grows exponentially.

The main objective of the Human Resources Management is to make sure the company has and retains employees with essential skills to accomplish the company's goals.

5 Main core function to Human Resources Management:

1. **Staffing** – the process of hiring, positioning and overseeing the employee's welfare in the

organization. It is making sure that you have the right type of people with the right type of skills to achieve the company's goals.

2. **Human Resources Development** – the process of developing your employees to maximize their effectiveness in their work and role for the company. This can be achieve by training, organizational appraisal and performance appraisals.

3. **Compensation and Benefit** – this is the Human Resources Management function which assure that employee receives the right wage in accordance to the Minimum Wage Law or bargains with the wage based on employee's appraisal. Human Resources Department will also make sure that the company gives the employee's benefit like Health Insurance, SSS, PAGIBIG, 13th month pays, and other Bonuses based on standard practice protocols as reiterated by Department of Labor and Employment.

4. **Safety and Health** – this function is about assuring that the employee's working condition are within safety standards and compliant with government regulations. These includes safety and health training programs.

5. **Employee and Labor relations** – During times when work related issues and problems arise, the Human Resources Department are the key people in representing the company in a collective bargaining agreement with the Union Representative. The Human Resource Department is also in-charge of handling employee to employee work relation grievances.

Compensations

Compensations are any form of payment to an employee for service rendered which came from the employer or company. It is comprised of salaries, benefits, incentives, and allowances.

- ✓ Salaries. It comprises the monthly payments and bonuses.
- ✓ Benefits. These are classified into quantifiable (e.g. medical leave, emergency leave, seminar sponsorship, company car, etc.) and non-quantifiable (e.g. employee of the month, retirement benefit, promptness award, and etc.)
- ✓ Incentives. These are additional remuneration based on target performance and output (e.g. profit sharing, sales bonuses, performance bonuses, etc.)
- ✓ Allowances. These are supplemental income to compensate for employees rendering additional duties or performing of specialized skilled labor for the sake of the company (e.g. Transportation allowances, uniform allowance, hazard pay, and etc.)

Why do we give compensation?

1. *To attract employees.*

Giving a generous compensation will attract the potential employees in your employee's pool. The more people in your employee's pool the more choices you have to get the best people on board.

2. To retain employees.

Giving good compensations will give you a better chance on retaining your employees for a longer period of time.

3. To motivate employees.

Good compensation can make your employees work harder particularly to achieve incentives like performance bonuses.

4. To introduce a new behavior.

If you need some of your key employee to take on new roles for the company, you should utilize position promotion strategy to increase their base pay so they would take on the challenge for the company.

5. **_As a form of recognition._**

   Employee's feel a sense of recognition for their work contribution, expertise and dedication for the company thru pay packages.

6. **_Elevate the company's reputation._**

   A company that pays good and generous compensation for their employee reflects the soundness and stability of the company.

Chapter 11

Financial Analysis and Forecasting

Financial Planning is an ongoing process that involves financial analysis to make sensible decisions about money matters of the business. This process includes analyzing financial flows, financial forecasting, investment decision, and financial strategy implementations.

Financial analysis refers to the process of analyzing the past, present and future financial well-being of a business.

The financial analysis includes the study of the Income statement, cash flow and balance sheet which can be reviewed from the previous chapter on financial data. In this chapter we will focus more on break-even analysis and financial ratio analysis.

> ## Break-even point analysis

It is the process used to determine the number of units (product / service) that your company has to sell to cover the whole operational cost of the business hence considering the sales break-even.

Formula:

Break-even point per unit (BEPU) = Fixed cost / (price per unit – variable cost)

Fixed cost are expense of the company that don't change over a relevant value of time (e.g. property, insurance, equipment, utilities and etc.) These are cost that don't change over production or are not affected by manufacturing cost.

Variable cost are expenses or cost of the company that are dependent on the number of units produced (e.g. raw material, assembly cost, direct labor, etc)

Table 11.1 Sample of Break-even point per unit

Manuel's Shoe Factory
Break-Even Point Analysis

FIXED COST: 100,000 PHP

Variable Cost per Pair of shoe = 200 PHP

Cost of a Pair of Shoe = 1000 PHP

BEPU=FC/(PRICE per unit –VC)

BEPU = 100,000 / (1000-200)

BEPU = 125 Units

BEPP or Break-Even Point in Pesos = BEPU x PRICE per unit

BEPP = 125 units x1000

BEPP = 125,000 pesos

Conclusion: a sale of 125 units can make the company a break-even in profit.

Anything higher that 125 unit sales is positive income and anything lower that 125 units sales is negative income.

If you think 125 unit is impossible to sell and that selling 100 units is more feasible, you have some optional variable adjustment to consider.

1. Reduce your fixed cost. (E.g. decrease your FC to 80,000)
2. Increase your price per unit (E.g. increase your PPU to 1200)
3. Reduce your VC in combination with other variable adjustment (E.g. Increase PPU by 1100 and reduce VC to 100)

➢ Financial Ratio Analysis

Financial ratios are accounting tools used by a business in the analysis of the financial well-being of a company. By understanding these ratios, we might be able to modify our financial directions to improve our strengths and work-on our weaknesses. There are numerous financial ratios but for the sake of simplicity, we will focus on only 4 types.

1. Liquidity ratios
2. Activity ratios
3. Profitability ratios
4. Financial Leverage ratios

Liquidity ratio.

They are financial tools to measures the ability of the company to pay its short-term obligations. They are important in the assessment of the company's financial health. They compare easily liquidated asset with short term obligation. The higher the ratio the better the capacity of the company to pay their short-term debt. Lower liquidity ratios are red flags for investors. The most commonly used are current ratio.

✓ Current ratio = current assets (assets that can be converted to cash with 12 months)/ current liabilities (debt that has to paid within 12 months)

Table 11.2 Current Ratio Example

Ed's delivery service balance sheet December 31, 2016	
Assets	

Cash	150,000
Account receivables	25,000
Inventories	75,000
Prepaid Expense	50,000
Net Fixed Assets	300,000
Total ASSETS	600,000
Liabilities and Owners equity	
Notes Payable	50,000
Accounts Payable	50,000
Accrued Liabilities	50,000
Long term debt	150,000
Total Liabilities	300,000
Owner's Equity	300,000
Total Liabilities and Owner's Equity	600,000

Current ratio = Current Assets /current Liabilities

Current Ratio = (150,000 + 25,000 + 75,000 + 50,000) / (50,000 + 50,000 + 50,000) = 300,000/150,000 = **2 or 2:1**

Conclusion: 2:1 is a good ratio that means the company has the capacity to pay short-term obligation

Remember:

> _Current assets_ are cash or any valuable properties that can reasonably converted to cash within a year. They include: Cash, account receivables (money to be received from customers), inventory (list of goods to be sold), prepaid expenses (future expenses that have paid in advance).
>
> _Current liabilities_ are amount due to paid to creditors with the year. They includes:
> Accounts payable (sum to paid to supplier), Accrued expenses (refers to operational expenses like payroll, overhead expense), taxes

Activity Ratio.

They are financial tool that are used to determine the ability of a business to convert available resources to cash. The speed of the conversion of resources to cash is reflective of the efficiency of the company. It is also called turnover ratio. There are many types of activity ratio but we will focus on the most important types. They are called the inventory turnover ratio and Working capital turnover ratio.

✓ Stock / Inventory turnover ratio.

This ratio measures the number of times an inventory turns into cash during the year.

Formula:

Inventory turnover ratio = cost of goods sold / [(inventory beginning +inventory end)/2]

Table 11.3 Example of inventory turnover ratio

Jim's Soap Factory Statement of Changes in Financial Position For year end Dec 31,2015		
	JAN 1, 2015	DEC 31, 2015
All Inventory	100,000.00	25,000.00
Total cost goods sold		300,000.00

Inventory turnover ratio = cost of goods sold / [(inventory beginning +inventory end)/2]

Inventory turnover ratio = 300,000 / [(100,000+25,000)/2]
Inventory turnover ratio = 300,000 / [125,000/2]

Inventory turnover ratio = 300,000 / 62,500
Inventory turnover ratio = 4.8 times

Conclusion: 4.8 time is not relevant unless you can compare it with other company of the same industry of soap factory.
Another strategy you can do is do a monthly or quarterly inventory turnover to be able to assess if your company's efficiency rate is improving.

✓ Working Capital turnover ratio.

It is a financial tool to measure the efficiency of the utilization of working capital that is spent on operation to revenue. This parameter is very important for financial investors who are intending to infuse financial capital on a business.

Formula:

Working Capital turnover = sales revenue / working capital

Working capital = current assets –current liabilities

Table 11.4 Example of Working Capital Turnover

Current assets are cash or any valuable properties that can reasonably converted to cash within a year. They include: Cash, account receivables (money to be received from customers), inventory (list of goods to be sold), prepaid expenses (future expenses that have paid in advance).

Current liabilities are amount due to paid to creditors with the year. They includes:
Accounts payable (sum to paid to supplier), Accrued expenses (refers to operational expenses like payroll, overhead expense), taxes

Ed's delivery service balance sheet December 31, 2016	
Assets	
Cash	150,000
Account receivables	25,000
Inventories	75,000
Prepaid Expense	50,000
Net Fixed Assets	300,000
Total ASSETS	600,000
Liabilities and Owners equity	
Notes Payable	50,000

Accounts Payable	50,000
Accrued Liabilities	50,000
Long term debt	150,000
Total Liabilities	300,000
Owner's Equity	300,000
Total Liabilities and Owner's Equity	600,000

(assuming we have a sales revenue of 300,000.00)

Working capital = Current Assets - current Liabilities
Working capital = (150,000 + 25,000 + 75,000 + 50,000) - (50,000 + 50,000 + 50,000) = 300,000-150,000 = 150,000
Working Capital turnover = sales revenue / working capital
Working Capital Turnover = 300,000 / 150,000
Conclusion: **2** is a good working capital turnover but it will be more relevant to compare it with other company in the same industry.

Profitability Ratio

They are financial tools that are used to measure the revenue generating capacity of a company with regards to sales, assets, and equities as to compare to the expenses and other relevant cost that incurred during a specific period of time. These ratio is reflective of the effectiveness of the company's management.

There 2 mostly used profitability ratio are the <u>net profit margin of sale</u> and <u>rate of return on equity.</u>

✓ <u>Net profit margin of sale.</u>

This will demonstrate how much of the company's profit will remain after all the expenses, interest, taxes, and dividends have been deducted to the company's total revenue.

Net profit margin % = (Net profit / gross sales) x 100%

Table 11.4 Example of net profit margin

Marie's Flower Shop		
Income statement		
For the Year ending Dec. 31, 2016		
Gross Annual Sales	800,000	
Less:		
Cost of Goods Sold		

Seeds	50,000	
Fertilizer	20,000	
Labor	200,000	
Mineralized	10,000	
Water		520,000
Gross Profit		
Less:		
SGA	60,000	
Rent	100,000	
Salary	50,000	
Insurance	30,000	
Utilities	20,000	
promotional		260,000
Operating income		
Less:	30,000	
Taxes		230,000
Net Profit:		

Net profit margin % = (Net profit / gross sales) x 100%

Net profit margin % =(230,000 / 800,000) x 100%

Net profit margin % = 28.75%

In conclusion: 28.75% is good range but the company should use this as a baseline or a barometer for management effectiveness in handling money.

✓ Rate of return on equity.
It is a reflection of how much profit can be generated for every peso of the shareholder's equity.

Formula:
Rate of return on equity %= (net income / average shareholder equity) x 100%

Table 11.5 Example of rate of return on equity

Example 1: Company A earned net income of ₱1,700,000 during the year ending march 31, 2011. The shareholders' equity on April 30, 2010 and March 31, 2011 was ₱14,000,000 and ₱16,000,000 respectively. Calculate its return on equity for the year ending March 31, 2011.

Solution:
average shareholder equity = (shareholder's equity 2010 + shareholder's equity 2011)/2
average shareholder equity = (14,000,000+16,000,000)/2
average shareholder equity = 15,000,000

Rate of return on equity %= (net income / average shareholder equity) x 100%

Rate of return on equity %= (1,700,000/ 15,000,000) x 100%
Rate of return on equity %= **11.3%**

In conclusion: _11.3%_ mean that for every peso invested you will make about 11 cents. It is a good figure but for it to be relevant, you should compare that with your competitor's ROE. To be able to map your progress you should be able to compare that with your company's ROE from previous years.

Financial Leverage ratios

These are ratio between the company's debt and equity hence when we say that the company is highly leveraged that only means that company has taken too much debt and loans.

There 2 mostly used Financial Leverage ratios are the <u>Debt - ratio</u> and <u>Debt - equity ratio.</u>

✓ <u>Debt Ratio</u>.

It is a financial tool that demonstrate the ability of a company to pays its liabilities with their assets. It will show us what percentage of the total assets are owned in loans.

Formula: Debt Ratio % = (Total liabilities / Total assets) x 100%

✓ Debt-Equity Ratio.

This ratio demonstrates the percentage of financing that comes from Banks or stockholders

Formula: Debt Equity Ratio % = (Liabilities / equity) x100%

Table 11.6 Example of Debt Ratio and Debt Equity Ratio

Ed's delivery service balance sheet December 31, 2016	
Assets	
Cash	150,000
Account receivables	25,000
Inventories	75,000
Prepaid Expense	50,000
Net Fixed Assets	300,000

Total ASSETS	<u>600,000</u>
Liabilities and Owners equity	
Notes Payable	50,000
Accounts Payable	50,000
Accrued Liabilities	50,000
Long term debt	<u>150,000</u>
Total Liabilities	300,000
Owner's Equity	<u>300,000</u>
Total Liabilities and Owner's Equity	<u>600,000</u>

Debt Ratio % = (Total liabilities / Total assets) x 100%

Debt Ratio % = (300,000 / 600,000) x 100%

<u>Debt Ratio % = 50%</u>

(Debt ratio Of 50% simple tells us that 50% of Ed's Delivery service assets can be allocated to pay the company's loan. Usually a company is in good condition if the Debt ratio is less than 50%)

Debt Equity Ratio %= (Liabilities / equity) x100%

Debt Equity Ratio % = (300,000 / 300,000) x100%

<u>Debt Equity Ratio % = 100%</u>

(Debt – equity ratio of 100% means that Ed's delivery service has equally financed there assets with Debt and Equity)

If the Debt-equity ratio is less than 100% means that company's assets are more financed by the shareholder and owners hence it show that company is in a better position to pay existing Debts.

If the Debt-equity ratio is more than 100% means that company's assets are more financed by the debt hence it show that it might be more challenging to pay existing Debts.

In applying for a bank loan, the bank will favor a company with Debt ratio of less than or equal to 50% and Debt-Equity ratio of less than or equal to 100% hence Ed's Delivery Service is in a fair to good position in securing a Bank loan.

Chapter 12.

Managing Operations

To better understand the basics of managing operations, we should first reflect on ourselves. We should try think of ourselves in terms of business operational process. We would be surprise that in our everyday life, we are trying to manage our daily lives in the same manner as business managers manage their business operations.

Table 12.1 Comparison between our everyday activities to business operational terms

You	Business terms
The way you speak and dress up	marketing
The way we manage relationships with our family members, friends, neighbor and classmates	Management / communications

Developing a plan to achieve our life goals, hopes and dreams	Strategy
Using your computer, smart phone, tablets, facebooks, etc	Information technology
Making enough money to buy a new phone, tablet, or food	Finance and accounting
Making food on time, going to school on time, going home on time, finishing your homework on time, even planning a trip with your friends.	Business operation

Business operation are basically management of systems that produce our product and services. Managing business operations is very important fundamental of entrepreneurship. The daily operations of a company determines the success and sustained success of a company.

Managing operations simply refers to the administration of a business practices towards the highest level of efficiency and standard, hence the end goal would be a better product / service at the most efficient process to maximize profit for the business. This efficiency can be achieve by producing more high quality product/services with less time, with less work and a fewer resources utilized.

The 6'M of business operations are the back bone in developing a good product / service, hence it is important that we understand the parts they play in operations.

➢ Manpower.

This are the management of manpower engaged in the transformation of resources to profit this includes production crew, sales people, administration, etc. do you have the right people for the job? Can you train your manpower to be the right people for the job?

➢ Method.

This refers to process of converting raw material or resource into finish product and goods hence the right production method is important in producing the correct and target end product. Do you know how to make the end product? Do you know the most efficient way to make the product without compromising quality? Can you innovate a more efficient method in manufacturing the ideal end product? Is your production method produce higher yield in lesser time?

➢ Machine.

This will refer to the hardware used in the processing of raw material or resources into finish product. It is interlinked with Method. We should always remember machine decrease defects in production. The more machine we have means the more consistent our product will be. This will lead lesser human factor error in production.

Do you have the right machine to do the Job?

➢ Materials.

It refers to the raw materials available to create a final product. Do you have a stable source of raw material? Can you substitute the raw material for something more naturally abundant and more accessible for your production demand without compromising quality?

➤ Measurement.

The process should be measurable either by speed of production, the number of deliverable product or sales output and quality parameters like number of defective end products manufactured. This will serve as a barometer for you to measure the efficiency, reliability, and quality control of an end product. For a process to be managed properly, the process should be observable and measurable.

➤ Money.

This is the component that deals with the financial flexibility of a company to catch up with the demand of the customer for the product and demands of the shareholders for profit. Does the company have enough money to hire more employees or buy more machine to catch up with the growing demand? Does the company have enough money for advertisement? Does the company have enough money to buy raw materials? Does the company have enough money to hire the right people for the job?

Input – Transformation – Output (ITO) Model

This model is the simplest paradigm for management control. We should familiarize ourselves with this model because you can adopt the ITO model in any situation of operation managements.

Figure 12.1 ITO MODEL OF OPERATION

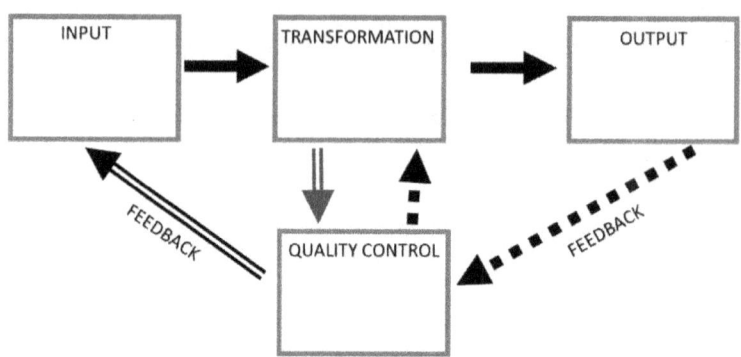

In figure 12.1 shows us how input of resources have to be transformed to product. In between these processes, we will achieve the right type of product with the help of feedback and quality control. A good example will demonstrated in Figure 12.2 regarding Production of dried mangoes snack.

Figure 12.2 Example of ITO model of a Dried Mango Factory

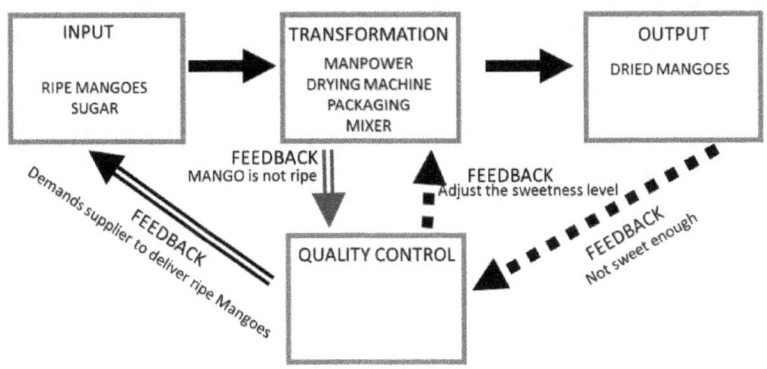

MAKING DRIED MANGO SNACKS

This model can be used from the simplest production line to multiple processing company like CAR production, where you interlink multiples of ITO operational models. This model can also be applicable to service type business from a simple barbershop to medical and surgical hospital units.

KANBAN

Prioritization of task is difficult things to do in management operations. As human beings we often confused to prioritize our task and even forget them sometime. A Japanese engineer for Toyota named Taichii Ohno invented KANBAN which is a system that improves manufacturing process of the Toyota Company. This Kanban is not only applicable for productions but to every aspect of management operation. This system utilizes visual cues in form of cards with written task and a board with the process of performing the each task. It will be explained further in the following example.

Example 12.1 How to do KANBAN

Step 1. It all start in a board with a title of the department and 4 column table with the following label incorporated inside.

Kanban for Dried Mangoes Snack

Backlog	New task	In progress	complete

Step 2. You and your team should collaborate and set up priorities of task for the flow of the operation. These task will be placed in the backlog column. Then assign tasks from the top being the most immediate need to bottom being the less immediate need.

Kanban Dried Mangoes Snack

Production Department

JULY 12, 2016

Backlog	New task	In progress	complete
Survey for marketing demand			
Order the adequate amount of			

ripe mangoes	
Slice the mangoes	
Dried the mangoes	
Mix the mangoes with adequate amount of sugar	
Dried mangoes Packaging	
Deliver the dried	

mangoes to retailer

Step 3. Move the task cards from the left side to right side column. Set a limit on the number of task not to overwhelm your employees. The Limit on task should just be enough to provide efficiency of the system. If a task is stuck in progress column, everybody should collaborate to find solution for the stuck task. Working with each other is very important in developing an efficient operating system. For this example we will set a maximum of 3 task limit and minimum limit of 1 task.

Kanban for Dried Mangoes Snack Production Department JULY 12, 2016			
Backlog	New task	In progress	complete
Mix the mangoes with adequate amount of sugar	Order the adequate amount of ripe mangoes	Survey for marketing demand	
Dried mangoes Packaging	Slice the mangoes		
Deliver the dried mangoes to retailer	Dried the mangoes		

Step 3. Move the task cards to the right column step by step. With a maximum of 3 task limit and minimum limit of 1 task per column, we will continue to this process until all the task are completed. Make sure that you time the completion of each task and all the column are utilized for purpose of efficiency.

Kanban Dried Mangoes Snack

Production Department

JULY 12, 2016

Backlog	New task	In progress	complete
	Mix the mangoes with adequate amount of sugar	Dried the mangoes (drying 200 sliced of mangoes for 3 hours in the machine)	Survey for marketing demand (100 pack of Dried mangoes needed)

	Dried mangoes Packaging		Order the adequate amount of ripe mangoes (200 mangoes needed to make 100 packs of dried mangoes)
	Deliver the dried mangoes to retailer		Slice the mangoes (200 piece of mangoes in 2.5 hours)

Advantages of KANBAN:

✓ Keeps your work flowing

- ✓ You are able to analyses which task needs improvement to keep the work system efficient. E.g. you might need more manpower or machine for certain task.
- ✓ You are able to compute for the company's production output hence you will not have complications with customer's demand expectations.
- ✓ You can save time by eliminating work redundancy.
- ✓ You can make sure that all the task are completed.

Chapter 13

Budget

What is a Budget?

It as an estimation of the revenue and expenditures over a specific period of time. It is re-evaluated periodically as to surplus budget (revenue > expenses), balanced budget (revenue = expenses) or Budget deficit (revenue < expenses).

What is a Master budget?

It is a set of financial statements and supporting schedule for the entire company. It is combination of a series of sub-budgets that will be interconnected to a master Budget.

Why do we need budget?

1. To be able to plan and control a company's activities related to revenue and expenses.

2. To be able to have a better understanding of your companies financial situation

3. To be able to compare our budget value and our actual costing hence we can come up with corrective actions to resolve it.

4. To be visualize if management's strategic plans like replacement, improvements and expansion can be financially feasible.

Stages of budget development:

1. Development stage – this is the stage where we coordinate with representative of every department to make a budget that is feasible and realistic for everyone to carry on strategies based on the objectives of the company. In this stage, everyone should collaborate in making priority strategies to achieve the company's objectives and sustainability.
-This also a stage where we receive feedback from the control department for strategy revision /improvement or re-implementation.

2. Budget planning stage - In this stage, we should put actual figures on cost and profit that can be involved in the implementation of priority strategies for the company. All of this figures, should be in consideration with the actual financial capabilities of the company.

3. Action Stage – This is the stage of actual implementation of the Budget Plan. This part is the execution of the planned strategies.

4. Control Stage – In this stage, we can compare the actual value yield from our budgeted value. We can surmise if we gone over-budget or under-budget hence these results will be reported back to the development team as feedback.

Figure 13.1 Stages of making a budget:

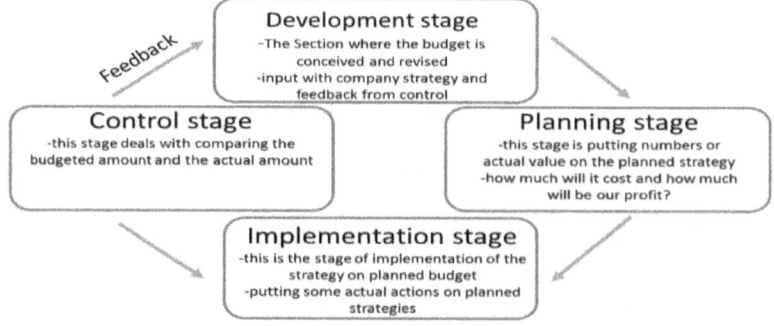

What are the benefit of Budgeting?

1. Managers will be forced to be active in planning for a Budget.
2. Manager will have to coordinate with other key members of other sections hence a group activity such planning a budget will be beneficial in creating camaraderie between the different department and in motivating for better compliance of the plan.
3. The budget can be used by managers as an evaluation benchmark for employee's performance based on the planned budget.

Three types major components of a master budget:

1. Operating budget.

   It is a budget that projects the sales of revenue, cost of goods sold, and operating expenses.
2. Capital Expenditures Budget.

   Budget that reflects the plans for purchasing property, plants, machines, and other long term assets.

3. Financial Budget.

   Budget that plans for raising cash and paying debts.

Figure 13.2 Parts of a master budget

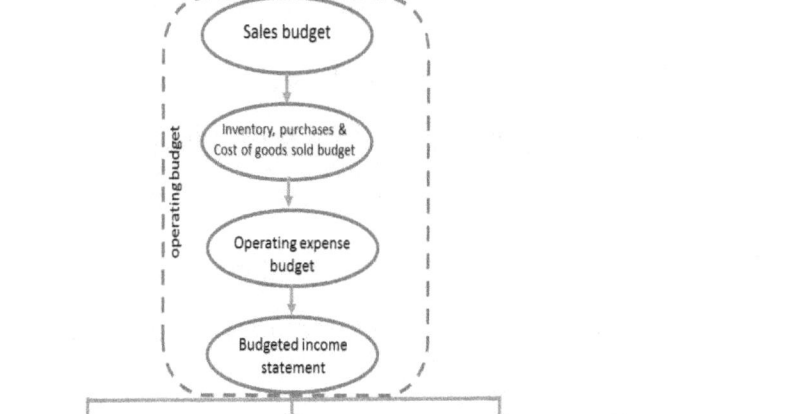

As you see from figure 13.2 the master budget is composed lower level budget and this lower level budget is composed of sub-lower level budget. To develop a master budget, we need serious effort on the part of the manager to coordinate with the different heads of the company and push thru massive effort on research to get the estimated figures close to the actual figures. My mission is to give you a clear mental picture of what a master budget and not to replace your accountants. Working closely with your accountant is a perfect scenario but if you are a budding entrepreneur with limit financial leverage, it would be difficult. Let me paint a picture of a master budget thru my example.

Table: 13.1 Example of Operating Budget

Parts of operating budget:
A. Sales Budget It is the pillar of the master budget. The starting line for the budget is estimating the sales of company over a period of time. To be able to estimate your sales projections, coordination with your sales team is ideal and proper uses of financial ratios like break even ratio is needed. (multiple the expected sales price from the expected goods purchased) Ex. Sale budget

Michael shoe factory

Sale budget report

April –July 2014

	April	May	June	July	Total
Cash sales (60%)	150,000	168,000	156,000	150,000	
Credit (40% Payable in 30 days)	100,000	112,000	104,000	100,000	
total	250,000	280,000	260,000	250,000	1,040,000

B. Inventory, purchases, and cost of goods sold budget

This budget contains cost of goods sold, purchases, and ending inventory.

Cost of goods sold are cost that are directly involved in the production of the end product. Usually cost of goods sold is presented as a certain % of the sales price which should be at par with the same industry.

<u>Purchases</u> are cash purchases made by the company (purchases = cost of goods sold + ending inventory − beginning inventory).

<u>Inventories</u> are goods in stock and they are affected by company policies. These policies dictate how much stock should be in the ending inventory every month as buffer for next month's projected sales.

Ex. Inventory, purchases and cost of goods sold budget (this is continuation of the sales budget with the following assumptions)

a) Cost of goods sold is 70% of the sales price.

b) Desired ending inventory is 20,000 + 80% of the next month

c) The Ending inventory becomes the beginning inventory of the following month

| Michael shoe factory |
| Inventory, purchases and cost of goods sold report |

April –July 2014

	April	May	June	July	total
Cost of goods sold (70% of sale)	175,000 (250,000 X 70%)	196,000 (280,000 x 70%)	182,000 (260,000 x 70%)	175,000 (250,000 X 70%)	728,000
+Desired ending inventory (20,000 +80% of COGS for next month)	176,000	165,600	160,000	200,000	
=Total inventory required	351,000	361,600	342,000	375,000	
-beginning inventory	(160,000)	(176,000)	(165,000)	(160,000)	
=Purchases	191,000	185,600	177,000	215,000	

Operating expenses budget

This budget will show the projected fixed and variable expense during the specific period. (Ex. rentals, salary, sales commissions, marketing expenses, insurances etc.)

Michael shoe factory
Operating expense budget report
April –July 2014

	April	May	June	July	total
Variable expense					
Commission expense	37,500	42,000	39,000	37,500	156,000
(15% of sales)	12,500	14,000	13,000	12,500	52,000
Miscellaneous expense (5% of sales)					
= total Variable expense	50,000	56,000	52,000	50,000	208,000
Fixed expense	12,500	12,500	12,500	12,500	50,000
Salary	12,000	12,000	12,000	12,000	48,000
expense	5000	5000	5000	5000	20,000

Rental expense Depreciation expense insurance	2000	2000	2000	2000	8000
= total fixed expense	31,500	31,500	31,500	31,500	126,000
total Operating Expense	**81,500**	**87,500**	**83,500**	**81,500**	**334,000**

D. Budget income statement

It is the combination of the sales budget, COGS budget, and operation expense budget. This budget will also include the term <u>Contribution Margin</u>.

Contribution margin = gross profit – variable expense – interest expense. It is the left-over amount that covers the fixed expense, then whatever amount remains after that will be considered profit.

<u>Interest expense</u> are non-operating expenses that incur as interest to barrowed funds like loans. (the figures will based on the previous examples)

Michael shoe factory
Budget Income Statement
April –July 2014

		Amount
Sale revenue		1,040,000
- COGS		728,000
=Gross profit		1,768,000
Variable expense		
Commission expense	156,000	
Miscellaneous expense	52,000	
-Total variable expense		208,000
= **contribution margin**		**1,560,000**
Fixed expense		
Salary	50,000	
Rentals	48,000	
Depreciation	20,000	
Insurance	8000	
-total fixed expense		126,000

=Operating Income		1,434,000
-interest expense		(2100)
=Net Income (loss)		1,431,900

Table: 13.2 Example of Financial Budget

Parts of financial budget
 	
  A. Cash budget
 	
     This budget projects estimated cash receipt and payments. It starts from the beginning cash balance and ends with the desired cash balance. It contains cash collections from clients or customers and cash payables. It is dependent on Operating Budget.
 	
     1. First let us compare our <u>Sale Budget</u> with our <u>Budgeted cash collections from customers</u>. Always remember sales is different from collected payments because in our example 40% of the sale budget per month is collectable after 30 days hence there is a difference between the actual sell per month and the cash collected per month.

Michael shoe factory

Sale budget report

April –July 2014

	April	May	June	July	Total
Cash sales (60%)	150,000	168,000	156,000	150,000	
Credit (40% Payable in 30 days)	100,000	112,000	104,000	100,000	
total	**250,000**	**280,000**	**260,000**	**250,000**	**1,040,000**

VS

Michael shoe factory

Budget cash collection from customers

April –July 2014

	April	May	June	July	total
Cash sales (60%)	150,000	168,000	156,000	150,000	
Credit (40%	104,000	100,000	112,000	104,000	

Payable in 30 days)					
total	260,000	268,000	268,000	254,000	1050,000

2. Let us compare COGS budget and Payment for purchases. In our example assuming the supplier will ask us to pay 50% now and 50% after 30 days.

Michael shoe factory					
Inventory, purchases and cost of goods sold report					
April –July 2014					
	April	May	June	July	total
Cost of goods sold (70% of sale)	175,000 (250,000 X 70%)	196,000 (280,000 x 70%)	182,000 (260,000 x 70%)	175,000 (250,000 X 70%)	728,000
+Desired ending inventory (20,000 +80% of	176,000	165,600	160,000	200,000	

COGS for next month)				
=Total inventory required	351,000	361,600	342,000	375,000
-beginning inventory	(160,000)	(176,000)	(165,000)	(160,000)
=Purchases	191,000	185,600	177,000	215,000

VS

Michael shoe factory

Payment of purchases

April –July 2014

	April	May	June	July	total
50% last months purchases	88,200	95,500	92,800	88,500	
50% this months purchases	95,500	92,800	88,500	107,500	
Total	183,700	188,300	181,300	196,000	749,300

3. Budgeted cash payment for operating expenses. We will try to use our sample operating expense and create a payment scheme with the following assumptions :

*50% of salary and commission are paid from the current month and 50% of the previous month.

*rent and miscellaneous are payed 100% on time

*depreciation is a non-cash expense so it will not be included

Michael shoe factory					
Operating expense budget report					
April –July 2014					
	April	May	June	July	total
Variable expense					
Commission expense	37,500	42,000	39,000	37,500	156,000
(15% of sales)	12,500	14,000	13,000	12,500	52,000

	April	May	June	July	
Miscellaneous expense (5% of sales)					
= total Variable expense	50,000	56,000	52,000	50,000	208,000
Fixed expense					
Salary expense	12,500	12,500	12,500	12,500	50,000
Rental expense	12,000	12,000	12,000	12,000	48,000
Depreciation	5000	5000	5000	5000	20,000
expense	2000	2000	2000	2000	8000
insurance					
= total fixed expense	31,500	31,500	31,500	31,500	126,000
total Operating Expense	**81,500**	**87,500**	**83,500**	**81,500**	**334,000**

VS

Michael shoe factory

Budgeted Cash Payment for Operating expense

April –July 2014

	April	May	June	July
Variable expense				
50% previous month	19,500	18,750	21,000	19,500
Commission expense	18,750	21,000	19,500	18,750
50% current month	12,500	14,000	13,000	12,500
Commission expense				

	April	May	June	July
Miscellaneous expense (5% of sales)				
= total Variable expense	50,750	53,750	53,500	50,750
Fixed expense				
50% previous month's	6,250	6,250	6,250	6,250
Salary	6,250	6,250	6,250	6,250
50% current month's	12,000	12,000	12,000	12,000
Salary				
Rental expense				
= total fixed expense	24,500	24,500	24,500	24,500
total Operating Expense	**75,250**	**78,250**	**78,000**	**75,250**

4. The Cash Budget

Now we put everything together. It will look something like this.

Michael shoe factory

Cash Budget

April –July 2014

	April	May	June	July
Beginning balance	300,400	262,050	272,700	312,100
Cash collection	260,000	268,000	268,000	254,000
Cash available	560,400	530,050	540,700	566,100

Cash payments				
Purchase inventory	183,700	188,300	181,300	196,000
Operating expenses	13,750	18,250	18,000	15,250
Purchase of delivery bike	50,000			
Total Cash Payment	247,450	206,550	199,300	211,250
(1) Ending cash balance before financing	312,950	323,500	341,400	354,850
Minimum desired cash balance	(40,000)	(40,000)	(40,000)	(40,000)
CASH EXCESS (Deficiency)	272,950	283,500	301,400	314,850
Financing of the cash deficiency				
Barrowing (80,000)	10,000	10,000	10,000	10,000
Principle payments (end of the month, at 10,000)	(900)	(800)	(700)	(600)

Interest expense (at 12% annually)				
(2) Total effect of financing	(10,900)	(10,800)	(10,700)	(10,600)
Ending cash (1) +(2)	262,050	272,700	312,100	304,250

B. Budgeted balance sheet

This budget demonstrates projected assets, liabilities, and Shareholder's equity.

C. Budgeted statement of cash flow

This budget demonstrate projected cash flow trends from operating, and financing activities.

After finishing the budget, the next challenge is getting your manager and employees to accept the budget. Here some of the ways to achieve this:

a. Close collaboration with managers and employees in creating the budget hence it will foster a sense of achievement and responsibility among the members of the company to follow the created budget.

b. You have to believe in your budget. If you don't believe it then no one will.

c. You should be able to demonstrate the value of the budget and provide reward incentive for the employee if the company's operation is within or near the created budget.

Chapter 14.

Risk Management

What is business Risk?

Business risk is the likelihood that the outcome of a business is either lower profits than expected or profit loss due to a number of factors. These factors can either be foreseen or unforeseen and controllable or uncontrollable factors.

➤ What are the major types of business risk?

a. *Strategic risk*

All good business usually have a good business plan as its backbone. Even with a good business plan that seems to have an update business strategy upon its conception may actually have an outdated strategy on the time of implementation. Strategic risk is actually using an outdated business strategy as a tool to reach your current goals. In this current day and age, we have to be current, relevant, dynamic and adoptable to effectively take our company to our target goal.

Example. In the case of Nokia cellphone which seems to be unstoppable during the late 1990's to the early 2008 was shattered in sales by a new technology called smart phones. Unable to adopt or compete with this new technology Nokia company profit went spiraling down.

b. *Compliance risk*

In starting and operating a business, we are obligated to follow the rules and regulation of the government. Considering that business and government are dynamic and nature, our compliance with these rules are often tested by new government regulation implemented on existing businesses or expanding business. Our challenge is to be always on our toes and update ourselves with any change in rules and policies. Non-compliance with the new policies will either mean bigger penalties or termination of business operations.

c. _Operational risk_

This type of risk pertains to internal inherit company risk. It usually pertains to the day to day operation of a business enterprise. This risk can originate from either the manpower or business processes. A good example of this would be a computer virus enters the server of a Business processing outsource company due to the download of file by one of the staff hence corrupting the main computer server which leads to stoppage of the business operation.

Operational risk can also happen due to external factors like environmental calamities like flooding due to typhoon with will halt all the business operation of a certain area.

d. _Financial risk_

This type of risk deals with financial loss due to unpredicted extra-cost in doing business and inability to collect existing payables. A good example to this is a sudden increase in dollar value over the Philippine peso. If we are trying to sell imported goods and paying dollars, sudden shift of dollar rate might greatly affect our business. Since we are collecting pesos from customers and paying our suppliers in dollars, there will be a bigger margin in the conversion of pesos to dollars hence we have to pay more. This always happens in our importation of oil. Another example would be, if 60% of sales collectible comes from a single company which undergone bankruptcy, we would possibly loss 60% of our sales collectible and future sales from this company.

e. *Reputational risk*

Remember that in business, reputation is everything. If the reputation of a company is damaged it will lead to clients loss and profit loss. If your company's reputation is damaged, customers would be wary to transact with you, your employees would feel demoralized and probably leave the company, sponsors will be hesitant sponsoring your events and your associate will want to cut their ties with you.

What will the different Business risk result? How can we lessen or mitigate the impact of this risk in our Business?

The different business risk will result on the following:

- Business interruptions
- All these business risk will affect your daily operation by stopping it or slowing it down hence it is important to plan a **recovery strategy** and invest in **Business interruption insurance**.
- Recovery strategy like trying to set up another remote location for operation is disaster happens. Business interruption insurance are very useful in disastrous situation.

Table 14.1 Example of business interruption insurances

Crop insurance – it is a form of insurance that covers crop loss due to natural disasters (typhoon, flood, drought, earthquake and etc.) and plant diseases as well as plant infestations.

Crime insurance – it is a type of insurance that covers business loss due to burglary, robbery, forgery, embezzlement and others

Fidelity bond – it is a type of insurance that covers business loss due to fraudulent act by specific people more particularly employees of the company.

- Loss of properties
- Like any property, your business property need to be secured and protected from unexpected events.
- Property insurances are useful in these events
- Some of these insurance includes fire insurances, act of God insurances, car insurances, marine insurances, and etc.

- Work place injuries – In any type of business particularly in the manufacturing units or construction unit, injuries in the work place are common hence a Department of Labor and Employment established Occupational Safety Health Center that seeks compliance businesses as a part of doing business. The Occupational Safety health centers provides programs like trainings and workshops that aims to increase productivity through a better working environment and mitigation economic loss secondary to accidents and disasters.
- The company should also provide employee's insurance like Philhealth and SSS benefit hence the employee will have wage replacement and medical insurance in case of an accident. Some companies would even provide HMO or Health Cards to employee for medical emergencies.

- Liabilities – Companies are also prone to lawsuits from accidental and unintended injuries, and other loss and damages brought about by the company's day to day activities.

- Strategic plan such as regular company audits can reduce undesirable situation that can lead to liabilities.

- In these type of event, General Liability insurance are useful in mitigating economic or business loss.

- Examples are Storekeeper Liability policy, Personal Liability Policy, Comprehensive General Liability policy, Product recall insurance, and etc.

- Security Breech – Information is power. Data loss and data theft are inherent risk in business and they are increasing more apparently in this electronic age of computers. This security breech can cripple a business and its operation.

-Strategic plans like strict implementation of limit internet access and updated computer firewalls are useful.

INDEX

About the Author

Dr. John Michael Lao, is a medical doctor, innovator, psychologist, business strategist, business consultant, serial entrepreneur, financial advocate, researcher, financial blogger and writer, stock market investor and analysist, musician, artist, anti-poverty advocate, motivational speaker, spiritual healer, economic enthusiast, and poet. He wrote multiple award winning Journals both in local and international events. He dedicated his medical practice to serve poor and marginalize segment of society. He believes that poverty is a disease of the mind and the cure is in increasing once financial intelligence thru financial education and empowerment.

STL

www.ingramcontent.com/pod-product-compliance
Lightning Source LLC
Chambersburg PA
CBHW071429180526
45170CB00001B/276